Cambridge Elements ≡

Elements in the Economics of Emerging Markets
edited by
Bruno S. Sergi
Harvard University

GLOBAL SOUTH LEADERSHIP STYLE

Strategies for Navigating Emerging Economies

Abel Femi Adekola
Wilkes University

Mona Pearl
Wilkes University

Bruno S. Sergi
Harvard University

Richard J. Muszynski III
Wilkes University

Shaftesbury Road, Cambridge CB2 8EA, United Kingdom

One Liberty Plaza, 20th Floor, New York, NY 10006, USA

477 Williamstown Road, Port Melbourne, VIC 3207, Australia

314–321, 3rd Floor, Plot 3, Splendor Forum, Jasola District Centre,
New Delhi – 110025, India

103 Penang Road, #05–06/07, Visioncrest Commercial, Singapore 238467

Cambridge University Press is part of Cambridge University Press & Assessment,
a department of the University of Cambridge.

We share the University's mission to contribute to society through the pursuit of
education, learning and research at the highest international levels of excellence.

www.cambridge.org
Information on this title: www.cambridge.org/9781009568661

DOI: 10.1017/9781009568678

When citing this work, please include a reference to the DOI 10.1017/9781009568678

First published 2024

A catalogue record for this publication is available from the British Library

ISBN 978-1-009-56866-1 Hardback
ISBN 978-1-009-56868-5 Paperback
ISSN 2631-8598 (online)
ISSN 2631-858X (print)

Global South Leadership Style

Strategies for Navigating Emerging Economies

Elements in the Economics of Emerging Markets

DOI: 10.1017/9781009568678
First published online: November 2024

Abel Femi Adekola
Wilkes University

Mona Pearl
Wilkes University

Bruno S. Sergi
Harvard University

Richard J. Muszynski III
Wilkes University

Author for correspondence: Mona Pearl, mona.pearl@wilkes.edu

Abstract: The Global South consists of emerging nations with increasing economic and political strengths, drawing attention to their unique leadership challenges and opportunities. Visionary leaders from the Global South leverage their political and economic influence to challenge the status quo and reshape the global order, exhibiting the potential for a transformational epoch defined by its unique and impactful experiences and creative energy. This Element introduces a novel approach by identifying regions as a unique leadership concept rather than a geographic classification, demonstrating distinctive leadership in development and dedication to a more sustainable global future. Our new Global South Leadership (GSL) Index identifies new players, agendas, and pathways to provide a framework for other nations that desire to adopt a path to improve their economic and social standing. The Element avoids labeling leaders and allows readers to interpret governance style and leadership dynamics for a more nuanced understanding.

Keywords: Global South, leadership, Global South Leadership (GSL) Index, emerging markets, global economic power shift

ISBNs: 9781009568661 (HB), 9781009568685 (PB), 9781009568678 (OC)
ISSNs: 2631-8598 (online), 2631-858X (print)

Contents

Introduction

The West has long been viewed as the dominant global economic and political leader. However, a notable and undeniable change is underway. The countries of the Global South – a rich and diverse collection of nations spanning Africa, Asia, and Latin America – are not just experiencing economic growth but a tremendous rise in economic and social standing. This economic growth, coupled with their cultural influence and a burgeoning sense of agency, is reshaping the global landscape. The economic development in the Global South is more than a statistic; it is a testimonial to its potential as a catalyst for dramatic change. While the term Global South evokes a complex and multifaceted image, the question becomes, is it a geographical designation, a shared historical experience, a dynamic geo-economic force, or a combination of these phenomenon? This Element addresses these questions and others by examining various definitions that have influenced our comprehension of this significant region. It also investigates this remarkable transformation, exploring the distinctive leadership styles and economic strengths that characterize the dynamic changes occurring in the Global South.

The element refrains from delving into the specifics of whether the leaders in this context exhibit democratic tendencies, authoritarian behaviors, or authoritative traits. It avoids categorizing or defining the nature of their governance and leadership methods in detail. Instead, the focus is left open to interpretation, allowing readers to draw their own conclusions about the characteristics and dynamics of the leadership depicted.

The Element's novel approach aims to inspire leaders within the Global South, recognizing the complexity of the issue and the limitations of a rigid North-South divide, emphasizing a new leadership style sweeping the world. In light of recent developments, Russia's presence and actions are a significant example. Russia's historical encounters with colonialism and resistance to Western hegemony resonate with many nations in the Global South. Russia, despite its high gross domestic product (GDP), faces wealth disparities and aligns with developing nations due to its economic strength, military power, and abundant natural resources. Its future relationship with other countries depends on the resolution of the Ukrainian conflict, economic direction, and its ability to establish itself as an alternative to Western influence.

Embarking on a voyage into the heart of the Global South, a region set to rewrite its global narrative on the global stage, is more than just a term; it reflects a complicated reality that transcends labeling. The Global South is a fertile ground for innovative leadership styles that transcend traditional Western models. This exploration aims to uncover the unique characteristics of various leaderships in the Global South and how leaders navigate diverse cultures, foster collaboration, and inspire action within a shared value context. The role of cultural values and social norms in shaping leadership in the Global South is not just a theoretical concept but a practical reality that leaders must navigate. By examining the effects of these factors on the region's leadership landscape, the purpose is to gain a more in-depth understanding of the unique challenges and opportunities that emerge within leadership in the Global South. The study results will facilitate the development of more efficient and culturally suitable leadership tactics for a rapidly evolving globe. The main emphasis is on nations from the Global South challenging the Global North in terms of economic and social standing; therefore, playing a more prominent role in global leadership. It is exceptionally fascinating to see how the Global South is increasingly asserting itself and becoming a prominent actor on the global scene. One of the main reasons for this transition is the rise of new leaders who are driving progress and influencing creative transformations.

This Element extensively examines the economic landscape in the Global South, by carefully evaluating several leadership indicators and indices that are used to assess development and progress and identify increasingly influential countries from the Global South. By examining economic growth indicators and effective trade policies, one may get valuable insights into the impact of Global South nations on the global economy. Understanding and analyzing these factors is not plainly important; however, it is imperative for any country hoping to stay ahead of the competition in this rapidly shifting economic landscape to adapt policies that positively influence these economic and social factors. The Global South's economic landscape is not just a backdrop but a dynamic and evolving entity that requires careful study and analysis.

Similarly, this work explores the possibilities that emerge when the unexplored capabilities of the Global South are acknowledged, and how leadership that transcends cultural barriers may foster connections and encourage global cooperation, creating a sense of worldwide solidarity. The correlation between GDP and leadership in the Global South is substantial, with significant implications and consequences. Effective leadership, particularly visionary leadership, is not only linked to economic progress, but also serves as a catalyst for it. Leaders who give priority to education, research and development, and innovation provide a stable environment for firms to operate and attract investment. Robust institutions, such as a well-functioning legal system and transparent bureaucracy, also contribute to a favorable business environment. Some aspiring nations such as South Korea and Singapore have achieved remarkable economic growth by combining strong leadership with investment in education, infrastructure development, and export-oriented industrialization.

However, the relationship between leadership and GDP is complex, since the Global South faces unique challenges such as resource scarcity, political instability, and social inequality. Leaders must adapt their strategies to these contexts and prioritize inclusive growth. The rise of Artificial Intelligence (AI) presents opportunities and challenges for leadership in the Global South. AI can aid leaders in data analysis and policy formulation, but ethical considerations and human oversight are essential. Strong leadership that fosters a stable environment, prioritizes innovation, and invests in human capital cannot just unlock the economic potential of the Global South but propel it toward becoming a significant player in the global economy. This prospective phenomenon is not only a possibility, but rather an attainable reality.

As a matter of fact, we need to understand the Global South as both a concept and a dynamic force that is actively transforming our world. It does this by exploring the definitions, leadership styles, and economic realities associated with the Global South. To promote a more inclusive and equitable global landscape, it is important to comprehend the leadership styles and economic influence of the Global South. Furthermore, we can establish a competitive economic and social environment that can serve as a model for non-Global South countries to observe and potentially adopt the mechanisms employed by the Global South. Witness the captivating and intellectually stimulating future of the Global South as it emerges into the forefront, commanding attention and inspiring liberation. Prepare to be amazed, inspired, and pushed to your limits by a transformative era that propels the Global South to become a beacon of inspiration.

The growth of the Global South calls into question long-held assumptions about power and progress. But what actually defines the Global South? Before drilling into its unique experiences and contributions, the next section will peel back the layers of meaning and definition. A more sophisticated picture of the Global South and its future trajectory may be gained, providing valuable tools for evaluation and research.

Leadership in the Global South is more than just a discussion; it is the driving force behind global influence. Visionary leaders emerge as unifying forces, bridging disparate styles and perspectives. They transform their countries by leveraging a potent combination of political and economic power. Their mission is to challenge the status quo and change the global order. These leaders see their countries not as passive observers, but as equal partners ready to make critical decisions and steer global affairs. The Global South Leadership (GSL) Index, debuted in this Element for the first time, aims to identify, pinpoint, and investigate the future of global leadership in the Global South, identifying new players, priorities, and directions, and guiding you through the formation of a new global future. Get ready to embark on this journey and meet the leaders of tomorrow.

Understanding the Global South: Definitions, Roots, Challenges, and Opportunities

The concept of the Global South is a complex and vague one, with its presence felt in various parts of the world. The term has gained widespread usage, with political leaders such as Joe Biden, Narendra Modi, Emmanuel Macron, and Xi Jinping incorporating it into their discourse.

However, the Global South is conspicuously missing from all maps and atlases. It's worth mentioning that numerous countries in the Global South are in the Northern Hemisphere. This underscores the idea of the current Element, which is that the Global South is defined by more than just geography. These geographical distortions may appear preposterous, but the idea of "the West" becomes as nonsensical when it includes Australia and New Zealand (The Economist, April 12, 2024).

In 2023, the growth of the Global South has become more visible in international governance, with the organization inviting six more nations to join (Argentina, Egypt, Ethiopia, Iran, Saudi Arabia, and the United Arab Emirates [UAE]). Could the expansion of Brazil, Russia, India, China and South Africa (BRICS) mark a turning point in the global landscape, ushering in a new era of economic and political influence? India's G20 presidency in 2023 also marked the first time in the group's history that the G20 troika consisted of developing countries. With South Africa scheduled to succeed Brazil in 2025, emerging economies would lead the G20 for four consecutive years, providing a historic opportunity to put the aspirations and concerns of the Global South at the center of the G20 and better shape the global agenda of sustainable development and inclusive growth. This ambition aligns well with the fact that 2023 is also the midpoint of the window for achieving the 2030 agenda. G20 India's achievement in this regard, was the idea of making the Global South attractive and progressive and no doubt more dominant, a place where massive digital transformations are taking place and where target-oriented climate action needs are occurring. This is all the more needed as the rise of the South and its growing impact on the twenty-first century international order has become increasingly evident (Policy Center for the New South, 2023).

However, the narrative of a prosperous Global South and the corollary of a more powerful bloc needs to be tested against reality. It is not always easy to identify Global South countries precisely, and they do not necessarily share the same views and aspirations. The political and economic landscape is heterogeneous, and strategic relations between countries with existing big powers are a consequential factor.

Global South: Defining the Term

The Global South is separated from the Global North by criteria such as economic development, living standards, and resource availability, among others. The approach has shifted from emphasizing development and cultural diversity to a more comprehensive focus on complex geopolitical power relations. The Global South refers to decolonized nations located south of old colonial centers of power, encompassing countries outside the Northern-Western core of political and economic interactions. It represents systemic inequalities from colonialism and imperialism, alternative sources of power, and resistance against Northern dominance and global hegemonic power. The Global South is often associated with the Group of seventy-seven (G-77) at the UN and countries referred to as "developing." The G-77 was established in 1964 by seventy-seven developing countries as part of the United Nations Conference on Trade and Development. Its institutional structure evolved over time, with Chapters in Geneva, Nairobi, Paris, Rome, Vienna, and Washington, DC. The original name was retained due to its historical significance. The G-77 is the largest intergovernmental organization of developing countries in the United Nations, enabling South countries to articulate and promote their collective economic interests, enhance their joint negotiating capacity on major international economic issues, and promote South-South Cooperation (SSC) for development. The organization has expanded to 134 members, but its original name remains significant (Group of 77, 2024).

The definition of the Global South is subject to variation depending on the specific situation and how it is interpreted (Haug, 2021). The subject matter encompasses the consequences of past wrongdoings committed via colonialism and imperialism, as well as the emergence of new forms of authority and understanding. The statement underscores the growing significance of these countries in different areas, as well as their mutual reliance. The Global South is often associated with socioeconomically disadvantaged areas, as shown by per capita income and the Human Development Index (HDI). The nations in question are grappling with a range of challenges, including poverty, famine, malnutrition, inadequate education, prevalent illness, and political instability (Kowalski, 2021). The notion of the Global South emphasizes the difficulties encountered by countries that are not categorized as high-income or advanced economies in fulfilling fundamental needs as a result of their common history of colonialism (Policy Center for the New South, 2023).

The Global South refers to a collection of nations, mostly located outside of the Western Hemisphere. Nevertheless, not all non-Western nations are included, which leaves the concept somewhat vague and sometimes contradictory. However, it offers valuable information and aligns with the concurrent growth of the countries it includes, and their aspiration to have a voice in international affairs and establish a non-Western type of leadership.

Academics frequently use the phrase Global South to describe nations and areas with diverse economic and cultural traits, making it difficult to categorize them under a single umbrella term. South America, Asia, Africa, and Oceania are examples of regions in the Global South with poor incomes and cultural or political marginalization. The notion arose from postcolonial conflicts and the separation between Western and non-Western states, and it describes parts of the world that suffer the impacts of restricted globalization as a result of their marginalization in the global system. It may also be interpreted as a metaphor for some parts of the U.S. and Russia, which are considered part of the more developed Global North, and nations in the Global South, such as Saudi Arabia and the UAE (Mignolo, 2011). The concept has gained prominence in scholarly publications, university research centers, and among activists throughout the world. While countries in the Global South are considered as far less developed than those in the Global North, they continue to play a vital role in supplying the required natural resources on which the Global North depends. Leaders of countries and businesses with worldwide influence may fail to prioritize the well-being of the great majority of the world's people, potentially denying them access to future prospects (Mignolo, 2011).

The European Union's (EU) decision of July 2024, to impose tariffs on Chinese electric cars (EVs) is one recent example. In its biggest trade case to date, the EU intends to levy tariffs of up to 37.6 percent on Chinese electric car imports, escalating tensions with Beijing. The four-month-long temporary tariffs are intended to stop an influx of low-cost EVs that were constructed with government subsidies. This was put into effect in July 2024 and emphasizes the difficulties of leadership in the globalized age. There is a review in November 2024, after which a decision for a five-year extension will be made. While the EU's commitment to a sustainable future through encouraging EV adoption is commendable, it seems at odds with the protectionist measures employed. The EU's domestic EV industry is not yet mature enough to compete with established Chinese manufacturers on price, pushing the EU toward protectionism. This traditional, inward-looking leadership style prioritizes immediate economic benefits for domestic players, raising concerns about its long-term efficacy in terms of strategic leadership.

The EU's current strategy might be flawed as it may stifle innovation, miss opportunities for collaboration, and increase consumer costs. Protectionist measures can create a sheltered environment for domestic industries, potentially reducing the incentive for European EV manufacturers to invest heavily in R&D. Additionally, they may miss out on potential fruitful collaborations with Chinese manufacturers, leading to faster breakthroughs in battery technology, charging infrastructure, and overall vehicle design.

Alternative approaches for sustainable leadership include increased investment in R&D, focusing on innovation within the domestic EV industry, and strategic partnerships with established manufacturers like China. By fostering a culture of creativity and leveraging Chinese expertise while fostering its own technological advancements, the EU can achieve its environmental goals while ensuring the long-term competitiveness of its domestic EV industry. This approach would position the EU as a leader in the green transportation revolution, paving the way for a more sustainable future.

The Global South, encompassing nations across Africa, Asia, and Latin America, is undergoing substantial economic expansion, altering the global terrain. This growth, coupled with their cultural impact and increasing empowerment, highlights their potential to drive substantial and transformative change on a global scale.

Roots

With ample opportunities for future growth as well as challenges related to the collective past, the Global South, a concept rooted in decolonization movements and the desire for a postcolonial international framework, is distinguished by unity among former colonial nations despite their diverse histories, cultural traditions, economic paths, and administrative systems.

With a plethora of future opportunities, as well as challenges related to the collective past, the Global South emerged from anti-colonial movements in the 20th century, including the Bandung Conference and the Non-Aligned Movement. The concept has evolved from being called the Third World to a more sophisticated term, avoiding historical baggage and hierarchical ranking systems, and now encompasses a broader understanding of political and economic differences and global interconnectedness, moving away from older labels. Although there is no universally accepted definition, the Global South refers to a collection of emerging countries that share certain features such as:

Exploring the physical location and underdeveloped countries. Although no longer strictly adhered to, the word originally referred to nations in the Southern Hemisphere, albeit this is not a distinguishing feature. The economic part of this term is frequently examined using GDP per capita, HDI, and poverty rates (Arrighi & Silver, 2005).

Exploring the notion of the Global South through the eyes of former colonies and their shared experiences. Several nations in the Global South have a colonial history, which has had a significant impact on their political and economic systems (Prashad, 2012). The Global South idea entails a shared knowledge of development challenges, unequal power distribution, and the pursuit of a more equitable global system (The South Centre, 2024).

The concept represents a shift in ideological and political stance, moving away from the term Third World to better encompass ongoing struggles related to colonialism's lasting impacts. The Global South promotes a vision of international relations emphasizing equality, freedom, and mutual respect, aiming to establish a new framework of power and subjectivity uninfluenced by colonial legacies. The region operates without a centralized structure or designated leadership, emphasizing international solidarity and shared responsibility. It critiques institutional and cultural norms influenced by colonialism and imperialism, advocating for a new global order centered on collective responsibility and ethical principles.

Shedding light on the obstacles developing countries face in their struggle against more industrialized powers, current trends include the creation of alliances among countries in different areas to counteract dominating powers such as China. Key themes and dominant narratives include colonial legacies, economic inequities, and opposition to empires. Intellectual movements such as subaltern studies and notions like "coloniality of power" have contributed significantly to our understanding of the Global South's history and challenges. The Global South refers to a complex set of economic, cultural, and political elements that impact behavior and interactions in this region (Dados & Cornell, 2012).

Influence

The globe is nearing the end of Western dominance, with 88 percent of the world's population residing in the Global South. At his Voice of Global South summit in January 2023, Narendra Modi, India's prime minister, said: "We, the Global South, have the largest stakes in the future ... As the eight decade-old model of global governance slowly changes, we should try to shape the emerging order." Many Global South countries, including South America, Africa, and Asia, are no longer passive participants on the world stage but acting independently of the West. This growing sense of Global South agency is evident in the fact that states representing 85 percent of the world's population have not imposed sanctions on Russia even though the majority of countries in the Global South condemned the illegal Russian invasion of Ukraine (Mahbubani, 2024).

The influence of the Global South in global affairs is on the rise as its economic production continues to grow. With nearly 60 percent of the global GDP and approximately 85 percent of the world's population, the Global South is becoming an increasingly significant player on the world stage. As a nation's power and influence increase, its desire for success also increases. For example, as a tremendously ambitious country, China aims to assume a prominent position on the world stage. China's economic power and ability to exert influence and pressure on other developing countries is currently only surpassed by that of the U.S. Several nations are increasingly eager to establish connections and exert their influence on governments in regions commonly referred to as the Global South. India's Prime Minister Modi takes great pride in highlighting India's significant role as a major trading partner and source of foreign direct investment for Africa. Additionally, India is deepening its connections with the Gulf states. Brazil, a powerhouse in agriculture, highlights the importance of ensuring food security. Turkish companies are actively involved in developing infrastructure projects across East Africa.

The Global South holds significant influence but also presents challenges in reaching consensus on various issues due to its vast diversity. It is difficult to maintain a consistent position on human rights when the group consists of democracies, absolute monarchies, hereditary dictatorships, and military-run governments. A group of countries consisting of economically disadvantaged countries reliant on energy imports and affluent nations with abundant oil resources faces difficulties in maintaining a unified position on the issue of climate change. In the short run, it is quite improbable that security cooperation will be realized throughout the spectrum of the BRICS-Plus countries, given the adversarial relationships between certain countries, such as Iran and Saudi Arabia or India and China.

Given the diversity of economic systems, ranging from authoritarian, government-controlled financial systems to more liberal ones, the concept of building robust and unequivocal financial linkages, such as a shared currency, becomes quite intricate.

Nonetheless, the novelty of this Element is to investigate the new global leadership concept focused on the distinct divide that has emerged within the Global South, distinguishing between economically disadvantaged and influential countries, different tiers of development within the Global South, and a fragmented Global South. This differentiation underscores the diverse challenges and circumstances experienced by countries, particularly with the ascent of nations like India and China. The impact of these two nations has been significant; although, it may not fully represent the realities faced by other areas such as Southeast Asia and sub-

Saharan Africa. China and India, as sovereign states in the Global South, are making significant contributions to the global economic landscape with remarkable speed.

China has experienced a tremendous economic change, rapidly emerging as a global economic powerhouse after the reforms implemented in the late 1970s with the introduction of the Open Door Policy by Deng Xiaoping. These changes signified a substantial transition from a centrally planned economy to a market-oriented economy, therefore attracting foreign investment and commerce. The period witnessed the formation of special economic zones, industrial modernization, and substantial infrastructural upgrades. As a consequence, China's GDP increased dramatically, pulling millions out of poverty and cementing the country's place as a major participant in the global economy.

China's dominance in international trade and manufacturing, as well as its technical competition with the U.S., has global repercussions for several sectors. Its size and influence make it a significant force on the world stage. China's Belt and Road Initiative officially launched in 2013 showcases its determination to establish itself as a prominent player in the global economy through a vast infrastructure development project. India has just begun to lay the groundwork for imitating China's model of fast economic expansion and modernization, led by Prime Minister Narendra Modi (recently reelected for a third term in June, 2024). Prime Minster Modi's administration has implemented a series of ambitious reforms to liberalize the economy, attract foreign investment, and improve infrastructure. This vision is centered on key programs like "Make in India," which supports manufacturing and local production, and "Digital India," which strives to improve the country's digital infrastructure and connections.

Furthermore, attempts to simplify corporate rules, promote talent development, and increase ease of doing business are part of a larger goal to convert India into a worldwide economic powerhouse. By adopting elements of China's economic approach, India hopes to accelerate its development trajectory, generate millions of employment, and considerably enhance its population's living standards. India is predicted to become the world's third-largest economy by 2027, with a nominal GDP of $3.4 trillion. The country has climbed to the fifth position with structural reforms, enhancing its macroeconomic landscape. India's GDP is set to reach $5 trillion within four years, with a target of nearly $10 trillion by 2030, predicting a 6 percent annual GDP growth rate over the next five years, surpassing most large economies (Laker, 2024).

The Global South, as a collective of emerging nations, is increasingly making its voice heard in global politics on various issues. China's Foreign

Minister Wang Yi has described the Global South as a key force for reform-ing the international order, and a source of hope as the world undergoes profound changes unseen in a century. However, it is less clear whether this broad grouping can translate shared concern into meaningful action. In order to accomplish this, it will need to manage internal differences and a global landscape characterized by significant power rivalry, notably the deteriorat-ing ties between the two dominant powers, China and the U.S.

The current competition underway in the Pacific Island Countries exemplifies this trend. As China's economic and security ties with these nations deepen, the U.S., along with its allies and partners, is intensifying its efforts to counterbal-ance China's influence by renewing engagement and opening new embassies, including in the Solomon Islands and Tonga. This deepening distrust between China and the U.S. is now affecting their relationships with many Global South countries, putting them in the uncomfortable position of having to make choices they didn't sign up for.

China and India are currently navigating challenging bilateral relations since normalizing their relations four decades ago. Both China and India have made attempts to bring Global South nations together, but not all countries will join the bloc. However, they will both play a major role in the Global South and will continue to do so in future expansion of the BRICS-Plus. The Global South bloc is confronting a multitude of issues subsequent to the Voice of the Global South Summit, which was held in India in November 2023. They emphasize that it is not appropriate for any nation to be forced to make a decision between combating poverty and protecting the environment. They advocate for the future of climate action to be guided by principles of fairness, climate justice, and the concept of "Common but Differentiated Responsibilities." Reaching a consensus on political rebalancing is a delicate task, particularly due to the oppos-ition and delay of China, a key member and supporter of the Global South, which also happens to be one of the five permanent members of the UN Security Council (UNSC) and is against any revisions to the UNSC reforms.

According to Brazil's President, Luiz Inácio Lula da Silva, there is a strong sense of unity within the Global South. Nevertheless, a common thread among countries in the Global South is their criticism of what they see as the domin-ance of the Western world. The Global South expresses deep concern over what it sees as a limited focus on Ukraine and unmet obligations regarding climate funding (Krishnan, 2024). South Africa's recent move to file a genocide com-plaint against Israel at the International Court of Justice in January 2024 is worth noting.

Challenges and Concerns

There is a concern that the concept of the Global South could potentially lead to the development of a complex form of nihilism. China may seek to exploit this idea by blending the notion of being a developing nation on the trajectory of a high-income country with anti-Western sentiments, thereby adopting an adversarial position against global liberal values (AP News, 2024). At the UN, China presents itself as a member of the Global South as an alternative to a Western model.

In the realm of international discourse, the Global South has gained significant attention. However, it is important to recognize that the concept of the Global South oversimplifies complex realities and fails to acknowledge the diverse economic interests, development paths, and political traditions that exist within these countries. The concept of the Global South involves understanding the locations where global futures are shaped through a process of disengagement from the colonial power structure. Decolonization is a voluntary process, not something that is imposed. This option can include regions in the southern part of the world and marginalized communities in the northern regions (for example, the southern states in the U.S.). On the other hand, numerous countries are situated below the equator and encompassed within the Global South. Our novel perspective challenges the traditional view of the Southern Hemisphere and instead includes a worldwide area consisting of developing and growing nations, known as the Global South, which provide raw materials to more industrialized countries. Essentially, we assert that the concept of the Global South goes beyond only geographical location. It encompasses an ideological viewpoint that sheds light on the unequal economic, political, and knowledge-based interactions within the global world order, as seen from the perspective of marginalized communities.

Opportunities and New Avenues

A fresh viewpoint is needed when examining the Global South in the context of globalization. López (2007) argues that our understanding of the Global South as the Third World or former colonies is antiquated. Globalization is also responsible for worldwide poverty, displacement, and environmental devastation. Examining the Global South as a unified entity enables one to transcend geographical and ideological boundaries. The Global South is a complex phenomenon that warrants a thorough examination in the context of globalization. It transcends geographical boundaries and necessitates a focus on marginalized and disenfranchised individuals. The Global South has witnessed the emergence of different transnational movements and ideologies that have frequently come into conflict with nationalist sentiments and struggled to establish enduring supranational identities. The ongoing conflicts within developing nations have a significant impact on global politics, which in turn questions the idea of a cohesive Global South. In addition, elites from non-Western regions have demonstrated a willingness to cooperate with the West in order to attain economic and security objectives. This further complicates the notion of a distinct division between the Global South and the Global North.

Moreover, it is evident that the countries in the Global South are experiencing substantial changes, characterized by certain notable trends. Undeniably, there are distinct factors that differentiate them from other regions. Despite ongoing disparities with other regions, numerous countries in the Global South have witnessed significant economic progress in recent years. This growth has been fueled by various factors such as industrialization, urbanization, and foreign investment (World Bank, 2023), although other changes are at stake. As these societies progress, it is crucial to acknowledge the significant influence of the growing middle class in driving the economies of developing regions. This particular group of individuals and customers has emerged as a significant driving force behind the economies of various nations. Consequently, we need to recognize and value their significant influence on these nations' future opportunities. Considering the requirements and ambitions of this growing group is of utmost importance, and it is essential to create possibilities that will benefit their communities. The substantial economic expansion in many countries in the Global South has led to the rise of a rapidly growing middle class, thus leading to shifts in spending patterns and social structures (OECD, 2022).

Furthermore, the Global South is witnessing a remarkable surge in technological progress, specifically regarding mobile phone usage and internet availability. These advancements have profoundly affected various aspects, such as communication, education, and economic prospects (International Telecommunication Union, ITU, 2023). Finally, the region is currently witnessing a rise in social movements and transitions toward democracy, with a focus on promoting equality, human rights, and environmental sustainability (UN DESA, 2023).

The Global South's economic leadership and the perceived demise of the West are subjects of an active and lively debate (Gray & Gills, 2016). There are diverse viewpoints about the possibilities of economic growth in the Global South, with some seeing it as a means to emancipation from the hegemony of the Global North. Conversely, several individuals see it as an integral component of the prevailing global capitalist growth paradigm. The intentions of elites in the Global South about their position on the dominating institutions of global capitalism are now a subject of continuous dispute. The current economic expansion in some parts of the globe has the capacity to alter the distribution of power and the governance of global organizations. However, we would like to point out that there are legitimate concerns about the Global North potentially influencing the Global South to join restructured global governance organizations, leading to the establishment of a consensus among a global elite about development. The conventional division of global power dynamics is becoming less relevant, particularly in light of China's rapid economic growth. This change in power dynamics emphasizes the importance of developing a deeper understanding of regional and global matters. Although the Global North-South framework may have its limitations, it can be a useful foundation for examining global issues. By critically analyzing these categories and tools, we can improve existing tools or create new frameworks to better understand the evolving global landscape.

Expanding on the distinguishing characteristics that constitute the Global South, the next section explores leadership challenges and opportunities, as well as their substantial impact on the global landscape, and sets the stage for the forthcoming evaluation and discourse on economic and cross-cultural leadership and diverse approaches.

The Significance of Leadership

Leadership in the Global South is seldom defined by a single concept or criteria. Instead, leaders typically navigate a complex interaction of several forces, ranging from political and economic constraints to social and cultural variables. These dynamics may include coping with various and sometimes fractured political landscapes, handling economic concerns such as poverty and unemployment, and resolving issues of corruption and governance. Leaders must also strike a balance between traditional cultural norms and values and contemporary influences and expectations from other nations. They often deal with external pressures from global powers and international organizations while attempting to protect national sovereignty and meet the needs and ambitions of their inhabitants. This multidimensional environment necessitates a flexible and adaptable leadership style capable of reacting to a wide range of internal and external problems and opportunities.

Thus, in order to assess the Global South's performance, we developed the Global South Leadership (GSL) Index tool (please refer to the methodology section), introduced for the first time in this Element, incorporating a holistic methodology for assessing and forecasting leadership trends. The leadership landscape has evolved to embrace a diverse array of viewpoints and backgrounds from throughout the globe. Leadership styles and tactics originating from countries in the Global South have a considerable effect on the worldwide stage. The Global South has gained a significant influence as it reevaluates leadership paradigms and pioneers its own approach. As these countries grow in economic and political power, their leadership styles impact global institutions and conventions. One example is SSC, which develops collective leadership to handle common concerns and negotiate more favorable terms with industrialized countries (United Nations Office for South-South Cooperation UNSSC, n. d.). Although other leadership concepts have a significant impact on the Global South, including ideology, religion, military, technology, economic, and cultural, all of which shape leadership in this region on a global scale, we choose to focus on two: economic and cross-cultural.

Economic and cross-cultural leadership are crucial for Global South countries' progress and prosperity. These regions, frequently marked by diverse cultures, complex sociopolitical environments, and growth economies, require leaders who can manage and harness these complexities to promote long-term prosperity. Economic leadership in the Global South addresses issues like poverty, infrastructure, and access to education and healthcare while positioning countries as global competitors. This requires leadership in the Global South to create policies and structures that stimulate economic activity, attract foreign investment, and encourage innovation. Hence, Global South leaders' objective is to promote economic growth, eliminate poverty, and enhance global market integration, aiming to overcome colonial stigma and join the global arena alongside developed nations. While each philosophy has distinct advantages, successful implementation necessitates a thorough understanding of historical and cultural circumstances. Leaders such as Nelson Mandela in South Africa and Lula da Silva in Brazil prioritized social welfare measures alongside economic development plans (Phiri, 2017).

This new strategy for leadership aims to establish a more equitable and inclusive economic landscape nationally, regionally, and on a broader global scale within specific regions.

Consequently, effective cross-cultural leadership is crucial for understanding and managing cultural complexities within and between nations. It involves comprehending diverse societies and countries' expectations of what is perceived as good leadership while gaining deeper insights into their leadership structures. It helps bridge gaps, foster inclusive environments, and build cohesive communities. Effective cross-cultural leadership reduces conflicts caused by ethnic, religious, or linguistic diversity, promotes societal harmony and stability, and facilitates collaboration with foreign partners, allowing the Global South to tap into global networks and resources, accelerating growth and innovation.

Solid economic and cross-cultural leadership impacts various sectors, including education, healthcare, and technology. Education leaders may create policies that promote access while simultaneously assuring quality and relevance, preparing the workforce for a global economy. High-performing healthcare leadership can drive improvements to service delivery, making it more accessible and equitable. Likewise, visionary technology leaders may foster an environment encouraging digital innovation, thereby closing the digital divide and integrating their economies into the global digital ecosystem. Furthermore, the Global South's success depends on leaders who can anticipate and adapt to global trends such as climate change, migration, and shifting economic power. Leaders who can communicate and interact across cultures are better positioned to negotiate favorable trade agreements, obtain foreign aid, and participate in international governance. This versatile and competent leadership is essential for ensuring that the Global South stays current with global trends and capitalizes on them for national and regional gain.

Finally, the value of economic and cross-cultural leadership in the Global South cannot be underscored. Leaders who succeed in these areas assist in transforming obstacles into opportunities, accelerating progress, and ensuring their countries' long-term development and prosperity. As the Global South grows, such leaders might play an increasingly important role in fostering a more inclusive and equitable global environment. As the Global South develops its own leadership models, it will be able to reimagine leadership on a global scale, promoting a more equitable and sustainable future for all.

The subsequent section will present the concepts of economic leadership, gaining a thorough grasp of the complex field of economics and its critical role for successfully navigating the Global South.

Economic Leadership in the Global South

We can think of the Global South as a globalized, marginalized set of nations that, while lacking power in some situations, are becoming more visible and prominent due to globalization. These countries are far from centers of power and wealth. On many levels, they are influenced by policies over which they have no control, requiring them to manage informality owing to exclusion from formal institutions (López, 2007). The Global South can be viewed as a dynamic process rather than a fixed category, stressing the inequities and power structures inherent in globalization while also giving an opportunity to challenge these systems. This is a chance to rectify injustices and create new methods of knowledge creation (Kloß, 2017) by tackling existing imbalances. This surfaces a controversial discussion over the West's decline and the historical role of rising powers (Gray

& Gills, 2016). Academics and activists are voicing support for the Global South's new transnational capitalism, which is being criticized as replicating the dominating Global North's established capitalist development policies. The field is divided between those who believe in the potential for the Global South economic development and those who advocate for emancipation from the Global North dominance, both of which represent neo-Third Worldist ideology. Nash (2003) defines Third Worldism as the discovery of powerful ideologies and movements emerging from formerly colonial nations in the mid twentieth century. It examines the critical contributions of these revolutionary ideas and their impact on modern society, emphasizing anti-colonialism and resistance to neocolonialism (indirect control by former colonizers), developing-country solidarity, and addressing issues such as poverty, underdevelopment, and marginalization in the global order. Furthermore, some may claim that the Global South's prosperity is overly reliant on the current global capitalist growth paradigm. If this worldview is not challenged and corrected, it may result in a global environmental catastrophe resulting from the exponential growth and advancement happening in these regions.

Challenging the Global Order

Controversy surrounds whether elites of the Global South and "rising powers" genuinely intend to challenge current relationships with the arbiters of dominant structures of global capitalist development or seek to support and reproduce these structures while altering their global position in the system and increasing their influence within the existing structures. Some may view the trajectory of rising economic growth, industrialization, and financial capacity as a step toward reshaping global power relations and reforming global governance institutions through the implementation of global economic norms and regulations. This trend may lead to the construction of a global elite agreement on development, creating a "fictional unity" around the concept of a globalized and open world economy.

In a 2023 interview with African Business, Lord Jim O'Neill, the creator of the BRIC moniker (originally designated to Brazil, Russia, India, and China in 2001), discussed the future of this economic bloc and its potential impact on Africa. While acknowledging that the economic performance of BRICS (since South Africa joined the group in 2010) has not met initial expectations, he emphasizes that these nations collectively now outperform the G7 (the G7, a group of leading industrialized nations, comprised initially of Canada, France, Germany, Italy, Japan, the United Kingdom, and the U.S.). Russia was formally asked to join in 1998, bringing the total number of members to eight. This move reflected a desire to strengthen commercial and political connections with Russia following the dissolution of the Soviet Union. However, this inclusion was short-lived. In 2014, the other G7 countries protested Russia's annexation of Crimea from Ukraine and barred Russia from attending the annual conference. The group reverted to the G7 format, indicating a substantial shift in the geopolitical situation. The EU is also a "non-enumerated member" in terms of economic size. Lord O'Neill goes on to say that the BRICS might potentially rival the G7's political power in the global arena (African Business, 2023). However, as Lord O'Neill points out, the BRICS has obstacles, such as a lack of agreement between China and India and the possibility that the U.S. will withdraw preferential status for BRICS members. O'Neill views a unified BRICS currency as unrealistic but expects renminbi and rupee to become dominant currencies, as BRICS prioritizes de-dollarization for intra-bloc commerce.

From BRICS to BRICS-Plus

The recent inclusion of Egypt, Ethiopia, Iran, Saudi Arabia, and the UAE in the BRICS group starting January 1, 2024 (Argentina's president, Milei, chose to pull Argentina out although the previous president agreed to join the BRICS extension) and now known as BRICS-Plus, is widely seen as a possible driver of a dramatic change in the global balance of power and leadership (Battle, 2024). The BRICS-Plus bloc presents a significant alternative to the global agenda defined by the U.S. and its allies since it aligns with the Global South's interests and will become more economically relevant over time (Bremmer, 2023). The Middle East and northeast Africa are increasingly disengaging from the U.S. and are prioritizing self-sufficiency. This may be attributed in part to the U.S.'s lack of interest toward energy and its position as a primary contender in energy production and exports. The U.S. is not a member of OPEC and instead competes with the organization. Consequently, the Middle East is reducing its alignment with the U.S., nevertheless, Saudi Arabia and the UAE have formed robust security alliances with the U.S., while simultaneously strengthening their partnerships with China and other nations that have substantial oil requirements. As a result, Saudi Arabia has engaged in diplomatic contact with China, urging all countries save Russia to join in the conflict with Ukraine. Bremmer (2023) predicts that the next phase of the extended BRICS-Plus would be highly favored by other sub-Saharan African nations. It is important to emphasize that BRICS-Plus is not a China-led rival to the G-7 since most of the member nations do not want China to have political leadership or to compete with the G-7. Indeed, their objective is to establish robust economic ties on a worldwide scale, and the existing economic structure is characterized by multipolarity rather than resembling the Cold War era. The BRICS-Plus will exert a more potent economic influence, facilitate more hedging in the Middle East, and enhance the ability to set the agenda in the global economy, as generally defined by the Global South. Nevertheless, this does not divide the globe into the G-7 and BRICS-Plus. China's achievement in diplomacy is of great importance, characterized by a nuanced and complex approach rather than overt aggression (Papa, 2024).

The BRICS-Plus countries currently account for 37.3 percent of the world GDP and 47 percent of the world population (IMF, 2023). The expansion reflects dissatisfaction with the current Western-dominated financial system and a desire for a more balanced and diverse global order. We can say with certainty that the growth of BRICS into BRICS-Plus, marks a significant shift toward a collective leadership approach on the global stage. This shift away from a single dominant power at the helm and toward a group-centric collaborative approach marks a new paradigm and a significant shift in global power relations. The BRICS-Plus countries are significant due to their large populations, GDP, and plentiful natural resources. They also establish alternative institutions, such as the New Development Bank (NDB), to counter the dominant role of the International Monetary Fund (IMF) and the World Bank.

Members of the BRICS-Plus have noted a significant inclination to conduct trade in their national currencies rather than the U.S. dollar. At the same time, the involvement of Saudi Arabia and the UAE is significant, considering their vast oil reserves and considerable wealth of funds. Another noticeable tendency is that BRICS-Plus countries prioritize physical and economic growth, industrialization, and low-cost labor exports as sustainable paths to wealth, reducing reliance on cheap labor, raw material exports, and the Western banking system. Battle (2024) makes a persuasive case for the West to cooperate with BRICS-Plus, emphasizing the possibility of a brighter future for all parties engaged in light of the West's diminishing strength and the growing diplomatic coordination among BRICS-Plus members in Southwest Asia. Consequently, these countries possess a significant potential to significantly alter the global geo-economic trajectory order (Battle, 2024).

This picture goes beyond a conventional bipolar world ruled by one superpower. Instead, BRICS-Plus signifies the concept of a multipolar international order in which a varied set of nations share power and leadership. BRICS-Plus promotes shared leadership among developing countries, fostering cooperation and collaboration, potentially leading to a more balanced global system and a stable international order. This approach fosters a broader diversity of perspectives, impacting global policy on critical issues like climate change, economic growth, and international security.

Global Traction and Influence

With the BRICS-Plus countries' apparent economic strength and distinct development styles, it is no surprise that countries in the Global South are gaining traction as major economic actors and critical players on the world stage. The winds of change are swirling throughout the global economic landscape. Countries once on the periphery are becoming significant economic powers and critical builders of the future global order. Their growing economic weight, vast resources, and thriving populations alter global power dynamics. As the world becomes more integrated, these nations rise to the occasion and make their voices known. Their efforts are invaluable and demonstrate their worth. While the term Global South is ambiguous, some propose abolishing it (Patrick, 2023).

As mentioned earlier, the Global South now includes increasingly influential and prosperous rising nations, and reliable predictions suggest that many more countries from the Global South will become similarly important in the future. Economic growth has increased the power of these nations. Several nations in the Global South have high GDP levels. The demands put forward by the countries of the Global South have instigated significant political and economic disruptions that the Western nations must adjust to. The countries' strength has been bolstered by the expansion of their economies. Regarding GDP adjusted for purchasing power parity (PPP), India is the world's third-largest economy (Mitra, 2023), followed by Indonesia and Brazil. Meanwhile, the G7's share of global GDP has decreased from 50.48 percent to 29.64 percent since 1980 to 2024, partly due to China's ascent and the most recent rise of the Global South (IMF, 2024).

Like representative nations of the Global North, the Global South is gradually asserting itself as a significant force shaping the global landscape rather than simply receiving international influence. The Global South actively influences global economic and political issues through its combined economic strength, vast resources, and growing political clout. One expression is a desire for forceful nonalignment between the U.S. and China. This is not the twentieth century's nonalignment but rather a fluctuating alliance based on the issue at hand.

The Impact of Conflict

Conflict alters and shapes the regions and the balance of power. The current example is Russia's invasion of Ukraine on February 24, 2022. While most developing countries oppose the invasion, they are unwilling to participate in sanctions despite the West's urging. Russia's invasion of Ukraine sent shockwaves around the world. Beyond the immediate humanitarian disaster, the conflict had far-reaching economic and geopolitical ramifications that are being felt today. Despite not being directly implicated, these effects have had a significant negative impact on the Global South. The implications for significant economic and social factors must be grasped, such as rising inflation, government actions to strengthen resilience, and potential adjustments in alignments between the BRICS-Plus bloc and the Global South are just a few of the long-term implications that will emerge. As the war progresses, continual analysis is critical to understanding its full impact on the world stage, particularly in the Global South. In addition to having a direct impact on inflation, government spending priorities, and geopolitical alliances between the BRICS-Plus group and the Global South, the Russia-Ukraine war caused severe disruptions in global supply systems, notably for basic commodities such as food and oil. Russia and Ukraine are major wheat, corn, and sunflower oil producers, accounting for nearly 30 percent of global wheat exports before the war (IMF, 2022).

Furthermore, Russia is a major energy producer influencing global oil and gas prices. The disruption in supply, combined with sanctions placed on Russia, caused a dramatic surge in commodity prices. The Russia-Ukraine conflict has increased world inflation by 1.3 percent points in 2022 (World Bank, 2023). This inflationary increase has had an impact on economies around the world, particularly those in the Global South, which rely significantly on imported food and fuel. The interruptions caused by the war, together with sanctions imposed on Russia, resulted in a significant spike in world commodity prices. According to the IMF, "[the war] was opined to push inflation to 8.7 percent for advanced economies and 9.4 percent for emerging markets and developing economies" (International Food Policy Research Institute, IFPRI, 2022). This inflationary increase has disproportionately affected low-income people and developing countries, many of whom were already dealing with rising food and energy prices before the war (Caldara, Conlisk, Iacoviello, & Penn, 2022). In reaction to growing inflation and supply chain disruptions, governments all around the world have shifted their public expenditure priorities. Many created social safety net initiatives to protect disadvantaged populations from the rising cost of living. Additionally, public spending on national security and defense has expanded dramatically. For example, numerous European countries have declared significant increases in defense budgets in reaction to the perceived threat posed by the war (The New York Times, 2023). This shift in spending priorities reflects an increasing emphasis on developing resilience to future geopolitical upheavals.

The increasing availability of resources, change in priorities, and the enforcement of policies are compelling leadership in the Global South to recognize and adapt to the changing direction of the global system that might have been compelled to expedite its progress due to the food crisis and inflation. The driving reason for the revival of the notion of the Global South is the process of including more nations. In fact, the resurgence of the Global South idea and its prominence may be attributed to their efforts to include other nations.

The conflict has also forced a rethinking of global power relations. The BRICS-Plus bloc, which has always positioned itself as a counterweight to Western domination, is in a perilous situation. Russia's activities have strained relations with other BRICS members, particularly India and South Africa, which have advocated for a diplomatic conclusion to the crisis. This disagreement inside the BRICS-Plus alliance could have far-reaching consequences for the Global South. Many developing countries rely on Russia and Western nations for commerce and investment, which could cause a schism between Russia or Western nations and other emerging markets. The battle may prompt these countries to broaden their alliances and reconsider their strategic alignments.

The conflict between Russia and Ukraine is only one example of international hostility that has harmed global ties and generated significant economic and political consequences for numerous countries. Another example is Southeast Asia's balancing of tight economic links with China and security relations with the U.S. There are barriers to the Global South playing a larger international political role. Individual countries' interests differ depending on their geographical location, size, natural resource endowment, and level of development. For example, China's Southeast Asian neighbors face a different scenario than South American countries inside the U.S. sphere of influence. Brazil has substantially greater levels of development than Vietnam. Similarly, a giant like India is unlikely to share the same world vision as a smaller country like Chile, resulting in the region's diversity of perceptions and worldviews.

A Glimpse into the Future: Growing Pains

As mentioned before, The Global South is establishing a fresh path in economic leadership, going beyond the paradigms previously established by a small group of developed countries. However, nations such as the BRICS-Plus bloc, Indonesia, Mexico, Nigeria, Türkiye, and others are emerging as key actors in the Global South. These countries have thriving economies, sizable populations, and an expanding global influence. They are determining the future of global trade, investment, and development. As a result, the growth of the Global South, a varied group of emerging countries with a common history of colonialism and a growing economic presence, is threatening the global status quo.

Despite its enormous potential, the Global South faces a fundamental challenge in the form of a lack of a unified leadership core, with the BRICS-Plus bloc emerging as a viable competitor for the leadership mantle. Internal conflicts restrict the bloc's ability to give coordinated leadership to the Global South. China's huge economic and political influence casts a long shadow, prompting concerns about its control, while other members, particularly India and South Africa, have taken a more cautious approach to foreign affairs, frequently contradicting China's viewpoint. Argentina's exclusion from the BRICS-Plus membership in late December 2023, as a result of the decision made by the incoming right-wing President Javier Milei, highlights the ideological diversity within the BRICS-Plus coalition. Mile's unconventional economic policies and social ideas may jeopardize efforts to provide a cohesive picture of the Global South. The absence of a single leader among the BRICS-Plus group does not rule out the potential of collective action in the Global South. Adding new members from a wider spectrum of political and economic systems may result in a more diverse and representative leadership structure. This might pave the way for shared aims and a more united voice on critical issues facing developing countries, such as climate change, trade policies, and access to development resources. Recent initiatives in the Global South highlight the prospect of a more collaborative leadership paradigm. The formation of the NDB by the BRICS-Plus bloc countries shows a coordinated effort to promote economic cooperation and development in the South, often known as SSC. Furthermore, the growing economic might of individual countries like India and Indonesia enables them to speak up and take the lead on certain issues.

The Global South is developing in a multifaceted manner, rather than as a single entity. While the BRICS-Plus group provides a credible framework for leadership, its internal dynamics and the rise of alternative voices paint a more nuanced picture. To attain authentic leadership in the Global South, governments must handle complexity, foster collaboration, and prioritize the region's shared interests. Argentina's political changes, led by President Javier Milei in December 2023, have created new viewpoints and a potential surge in populism across the Global South. This, combined with the sustained relevance of regional powers like Brazil, creates a volatile and unpredictable situation, making the future likely to be chaotic and unpredictable (Miller, 2024).

However, by focusing efforts on common goals and inclusive institutions, the Global South has the potential to build a more coherent and influential voice in the global arena.

Furthermore, the breadth and variety of the Global South provide major challenges. These regions are characterized by varying economic growth, political viewpoints, and geopolitical objectives, making it difficult for a single entity to have complete dominance. The Element suggests a novel approach, headed by the BRICS-Plus, emphasizing a new type of leadership. Morever, the BRICS-Plus partnership has sparked debate. China's booming economy and military may cast a long shadow over the other countries in the Global South, raising fears about its ability to dominate the region. Other BRICS-Plus countries, particularly India, have expressed opposition to being treated as mere Chinese satellites (The BRICS Post, 2024).

The debate surrounding the expansion of the BRICS-Plus bloc is multifaceted and influenced by various perspectives. Proponents argue that the inclusion of more countries could challenge Western dominance in global affairs, as the combined economic strength of BRICS countries surpasses that of the G7. The group's size and population suggest its growing significance on the world stage, potentially influencing global agendas and policies, particularly in development issues affecting the Global South. However, skeptics raise concerns about potential challenges of cohesion within the expanded BRICS bloc, as the inclusion of countries with varying political, economic, and social interests could lead to internal tensions and hinder consensus on key issues. This fragmentation may undermine the effectiveness of BRICS-Plus as a unified force for change and limit its ability to translate economic strength into meaningful global influence. The trajectory of BRICS-Plus and its impact on global dynamics will depend on how effectively its members navigate internal differences, forge common ground, and leverage their collective strengths to advance shared objectives.

At a Crossroad

The Global South is at a crossroads. While the absence of a single leader may impede some forms of collective action, it also provides an opportunity for a more inclusive and collaborative approach to leadership. By promoting cooperation and harnessing individual members' capabilities, the Global South can traverse the complexity of the international stage and chart a more solid course for the future. On paper, the BRICS-Plus group is a strong economic and political force, with a combined population of over four billion people and a sizable share of global GDP. However, various issues limit the bloc's ability to operate as a single leader. The admission of China, which has significant economic and political strength, has generated fears about group dominance. Smaller members may be unwilling to speak out for fear of China's influence. Furthermore, the recently expanded BRICS-Plus alliance broadens its interests, potentially complicating consensus-building (The BRICS Post, 2024). With the BRICS-Plus group encountering internal constraints and new voices gaining strength, the Global South's leadership conundrum becomes even more complicated.

The fundamental issue is navigating this variety while establishing a sense of collaborative action. This may have various shared goals:

Prioritizing shared interests, such as climate change, global trade, and sustainable development, can foster collaboration between the Global South and the international community.

Creating inclusive regional organizations that reflect the Global South's different political and economic realities can lead to more collaboration in addressing common concerns.

Encouraging economic and intellectual interaction among nations in the Global South can boost economic growth and reduce reliance on conventional power systems.

It is vital to note that leadership in the Global South does not necessarily belong to any particular regional bloc or nation. New and novel forms of cooperation and partnership may arise as developing countries seek progress. These countries can achieve their common aims and promote positive change by working together and exploring new ideas. Regional groups like the African Union and the Association of Southeast Asian Nations (ASEAN) might play a larger role in establishing regional agendas and advocating for the Global South on a global scale.

In Search for Leadership

The ongoing hunt for successful leadership among Global South countries has yet to yield a definite conclusion. The BRICS-Plus alliance enhances the bloc's participation, but its internal dynamics and recent expansion pose challenges, particularly considering the changes within the bloc. Additionally, the rise of populist movements and the growing relevance of regional organizations point to a more complicated leadership landscape. Multiple elements will form the Global South's leadership, with no single entity wielding disproportionate power. If the Global South wishes to strike a balance between the U.S. and China by drawing resources from both countries, China, as a leadership model is a contradiction.

Until a homegrown leadership arises, the Global South cannot participate in active nonalignment. The ramifications of a significantly stronger Global South can be grasped by examining the demands of Global South-affiliated organizations, such as the expanded BRICS-Plus bloc and the Group of 77.

The Global South advocates for increased representation in existing international institutions such as the IMF, the World Bank, and the UN Security Council. Furthermore, we contend that resources should not only be distributed more equitably but also be made transparent and efficiently used, therefore significantly reducing the misallocation of financial and other resources. The proposal for a "loss and damage" fund is being explored in international climate negotiations. The region is a powerful international force, necessitating strong leadership that comprehends global power dynamics and cultural distinctions. The newly developed GSL Index, introduced for the first time in this Element, provides a framework for leadership across nations and cultures, which is essential for navigating the region's different landscapes and cultivating collaboration, trust, and long-term solutions to global concerns. The complexity of leading across cultures underscores the need to understand these nuances. The following section will present methods and frameworks for assessing cross-cultural leadership, preparing leaders to traverse the cultural nuances of the Global South, bridge divisions, create cooperation, and achieve global success in a dynamic and interconnected world.

Cross-Cultural Leadership in an Evolving Global South

This section presents the complex relationship of culture, business globalization, and leadership in the Global South, emphasizing its impact on leadership styles.

Culture, a dynamic, and constantly evolving concept encompasses the shared beliefs, values, practices, and social institutions that define a particular community. It shapes how people interact, perceive the world, and approach leadership, and as Hofstede (1991, p. 5) states, culture is "the collective programming of the mind which distinguishes the members of one group or category of people from another." It went on to state that culture is "a collective phenomenon because it is at least partly shared with people who live or lived within the same social environment, which is where it was learned." Globalization, on the other hand, refers to the interconnectedness of economies, societies, and cultures across the world. This interconnectedness is driven by factors such as trade, investment, information technology, and the movement of people. According to Adekola and Sergi (2016), the term Global South emerged in the 1980s and refers to developing countries, often characterized by historical colonialism and economic dependence.

While globalization has a long history, its recent acceleration has significantly impacted the Global South. Marshall McLuhan's concept of the "global village" aptly captures this phenomenon, highlighting the interconnectedness facilitated by technology and communication. This intensifies interactions and interdependence between nations and cultures, necessitating new leadership strategies. Regionalization, where nations within a particular area collaborate economically, can also result from globalization.

Leadership styles in the Global South, a region with a unique and evolving leadership landscape, have traditionally been influenced by Fordism, a mass-production model focused on standardized goods for domestic markets. However, with the rise of globalization and increased competition, this model has become less relevant. Post-Fordism and neo-Fordism characterize the current system, where capital flows freely across borders and production shifts to lower-cost locations. This necessitates leaders who can navigate these complexities, fostering innovation and adaptability within a globalized context. Several factors contribute to the unique leadership landscape in the Global South, making it a fascinating area of study. These include regional trade agreements like United States-Mexico-Canada Agreement (USMCA) and the EU, the rapid rise of newly industrialized countries, and the economic reforms undertaken by China. Additionally, the end of the Cold War and the expanding role of international corporations have significantly impacted the flow of capital and investment, creating new leadership opportunities (Adekola & Sergi, 2016).

Culture plays a crucial role in shaping leadership styles within the Global South. Understanding cultural values and traditions is essential for effective leadership in these regions. For instance, cultures emphasizing collectivism might require leaders who prioritize consensus-building and collaboration, while individualistic cultures might favor more decisive and assertive leadership styles emanating from the value of a single decision-maker.

Cross-cultural leadership has been defined as bridging diverse cultures inside existing organizations or across transnational business relationships (Caligiuri & Tarique, 2012; Javidan et al., 2017). However, a more comprehensive approach is required to account for the reality that the Global South is not just a passive recipient of leadership theories but an active contributor to the field. It is emerging as an economic and cultural powerhouse, challenging the conventional perspectives on cultural development. There is a need to re-examine the relationship between culture and society and the need for new evaluation models and visions of social relations. The Global South's potential to produce a new understanding of equality and noncoercive forms of exchange in cross-cultural dialogues is a beacon of hope and inspiration in the field of leadership studies.

Additionally, basic assumptions need to be changed due to the complexities of understanding its distinctiveness beyond deterministic and paternalistic models. Other issues are the tensions and contradictions within the concept of cosmopolitanism from below and the significance of specifying an originating locus for a transversal form of cosmopolitanism. Lastly, challenges and rifts exist between the conceptual claims about the Global South and the actual social transformations (Papastergiadis, 2017).

Brummer (2021) posits that personality theory in psychology, primarily developed by Western scholars, has been integrated into analytical constructs to profiles of Western leaders. However, many non-Western leaders operate in different decision-making environments, which can impact their leadership style and decision-making processes. Thus, the ability to culturally contextualize decision-making processes and understand the root causes for certain decisions is not just a theoretical concept but a practical necessity rooted in the cultural makeup of the Global South as a whole, but mainly in the different nations with their diverse histories. This approach is crucial for effective leadership in the Global South, highlighting the urgency and importance of a global perspective. The states of the Global South vary in terms of size, resources, history, regime type, integration into the world economy, and external relationships. Many Global South States exhibit unfinished State-building processes, leading to State weakness and challenges in foreign policymaking and economic leadership. This weakness of the State is linked to issues of authority, legitimacy, and regime security, impacting State survival. The lack of consolidated statehood in the Global South can lead to internal and external regime challenges. Additionally, the dependency on the international capitalist core and external penetration by global powers further compromises the autonomy and sovereignty of Global South States, limiting their room for maneuver in decision-making (Brummer, 2021).

Gaining insight into power dynamics is a crucial element of effective leadership. Leaders have to possess the ability to skillfully negotiate the complex dynamics of power that have evolved over time and the lasting effects of colonialism. In order to achieve success, it is essential to adopt a strategy that challenges Western perspectives and promote local system knowledge. According to Earley and Mosakowski (2004), there is a fundamental need to understand the diversity of regional cultures and ethnicities. Indigenous knowledge is a critical component of good leadership in the South. Adopting a culturally varied perspective is vital. To create teamwork and unity, leaders must transcend these barriers. Another factor is the importance of sustainability and social justice: along with economic growth, many leaders in the Global South prioritize social justice and sustainability. This necessitates innovative solutions that consider the needs of the environment and the surrounding populations (UNDP, 2023).

It is also important to understand contextual intelligence. Thus, being a successful leader requires a thorough knowledge of the Global South's social, economic, and environmental state. Among these are efforts to address local issues such as resource scarcity and social disparities. Numerous problems and obstacles may interfere with successful and effective leadership in the Global South. One is the neocolonial practices and their traditions embedded in the institutions. This implies the likelihood of neocolonial practices being perpetuated within organizations, as seen by accepting Western patterns without regard for local realities (Prashad, 2012). Furthermore, due to gender inequality, women continue to be underrepresented in positions of power across the Global South. Addressing gender disparities is an absolute requirement for equitable and sustainable development (World Bank, 2023).

Additionally, individuals in the Global South might have had comparable experiences; some variables might make it challenging to foster collaboration and information sharing within the region. These reasons include historical rivalry, physical limits, level of economic development, and linguistic barriers, to name a few. However, collaboration, which is prone to division, also holds a promise for the future – with the initiative of the SSC. The Global South is an ideological expression of the concerns facing developing regions, which are increasingly diverse in economic and political experience.

Traditionally, policymakers and scholars have used the term SSC to describe the exchange of resources, technology, and expertise between the countries of the Global South. The Global South is making increasingly significant contributions to global development. The economic and geopolitical relevance of many countries has grown. In the past, SSC focused on sharing knowledge and building capacities. Still, the countries of the Global South and new financial institutions have lately shown a growing involvement in the advancement of a financial system. This collaboration pertains to the enduring historical effort of emancipating people and countries from the vestiges of colonialism, poverty, oppression, and underdevelopment. The notion of cooperation becomes the primary framework and set of actions for accomplishing significant historical transformation by promoting mutual benefit and solidarity among groups that are seen to be disadvantaged within the global system. This conveys the hope that these disadvantaged communities can achieve cooperation through the development sector and their mutual assistance to each other. The entire world order is transformed to reflect their shared interests from the domination of the Global North countries.

There is a growing emphasis on collaboration among Global South nations for knowledge transfer, joint ventures, and international collective bargaining strength. Another important aspect is the use of digital technology, playing an essential role in developing cross-cultural leadership. This impact facilitates communication, information sharing, and virtual collaboration across borders (ITU, 2023). When considering leadership in the Global South, philosophy and practice must be contextualized, grasping the full extent of understanding leadership in the Global South, focusing on the importance of context and power dynamics.

Advancing into the future, we can observe new prospects for the Global South. First is grassroots leadership. Local leaders and social entrepreneurs are increasingly shaping the Global South's development agenda, focusing on community empowerment and grassroots solutions (UN DESA). The rise of the Global South necessitates a shift in leadership paradigms. Leaders must be able to navigate the complexities of globalization while remaining sensitive to local cultures. By leveraging cultural strengths and fostering innovation, leaders in the Global South can create a more prosperous and equitable future for their nations. Having explored the multifaceted nature of the Global South – its diverse definitions, burgeoning economic influence, and unique cross-cultural leadership styles – now turning attention to a crucial question of effectively evaluating leadership within this dynamic region. This section probes into a robust methodology designed to assess leadership in the Global South, ultimately developing a valuable tool for opportunity identification, assessment, and planning.

Assessing leadership, regardless of the context, is a difficult undertaking. The challenge of defining effective leadership in the Global South is multifaceted. Traditional leadership models, often rooted in Western ideals, may not accurately capture the nuances of leadership in the Global South. Leadership might be less about individual charisma and more about fostering collective action, building trust across cultural divides, and navigating complex social and political landscapes.

A key aspect of the methodology we deployed is accounting for this fundamental distinction. Instead of focusing solely on individual leaders, it examines the larger leadership ecosystem within a region or nation. This ecosystem includes formal leaders in government or business and social entrepreneurs, community organizers, and other agents of change shaping the Global South's trajectory. This leadership framework offers a unique and comprehensive analysis by scrutinizing leadership from multiple angles. By examining various perspectives, the framework thoroughly explains what constitutes effective leadership in the Global South. This analysis unlocks valuable insights that empower individuals and organizations to make informed decisions. This framework considers:

- Economic Leadership: This dimension assesses how leaders promote economic growth, foster innovation, and address issues of poverty and inequality. Key metrics might include GDP growth rates, job creation, and advancements in social safety nets.
- Cross-Cultural Leadership: Here, the focus is on how leaders navigate diverse cultural settings, build community trust, including cultural interpretation of ethical dimensions, and promote social cohesion. Evaluating communication styles, conflict resolution strategies, and inclusivity measures are essential components.

A multidimensional approach to leadership analysis, as outlined in this framework, facilitates the creation of a practical tool for evaluating leadership in the Global South. This tool could empower various stakeholders, including:

- Developing nations: To assess their leadership strengths and weaknesses, identify areas for improvement, and benchmark their progress against other countries in the region.
- International development organizations: To tailor their strategies and interventions to specific contexts, ensuring that their support aligns with the leadership priorities of recipient countries.
- Investors and businesses: To identify emerging economic opportunities in the Global South, evaluate the leadership and governance environment within particular countries, and make informed investment decisions.

This methodology for evaluating leadership in the Global South and developing a practical assessment tool offers a valuable contribution to understanding leadership within this dynamic region. Moving beyond traditional models and considering the Global South's unique social, cultural, and economic realities, we can gain a more nuanced perspective on how leadership shapes opportunities for progress and development. This framework and tool are not static. This methodology should adapt to contemporary trends and challenges as the Global South evolves. Only through ongoing analysis and adaptation can the dynamic nature of leadership within the Global South accurately be captured.

Methodology: From Evaluation to Opportunity

The methodology applied that resulted in the GSL Index instrument is extensive and offers a novel path to finding and evaluating leadership. This instrument provides an adaptable instrument for discovering opportunities, assessing, strategizing, and making necessary preparations. By evaluating leadership potential across key dimensions, we can identify current and future rising leaders, anticipate future challenges, and develop targeted actions and support mechanisms. Moreover, this instrument can be used by various stakeholders, including:

International development organizations. By identifying strong leaders within the Global South, development organizations can collaborate more effectively with local partners, ensuring that initiatives are culturally appropriate and address timely and relevant needs.

Private sector investors. Investing in regions with solid leadership paves the way for a more stable and predictable business environment. This methodology can help investors identify promising markets with leaders committed to sustainable growth and economic development, helping determine foreign direct investment.

Civil society organizations. Effective leadership fosters a vibrant civil society. This methodology can empower civil society organizations to identify and support leaders who promote transparency, accountability, and democratic values.

Methodology: The Rationale

The leadership index we developed, the GSL Index, is a composite of several approaches. Economic size, trade balance, currency strength, innovation rankings, and global governance indicators are some of the most common approaches; however, individually, they do not capture the full extent of the potential and do not provide a complete picture. Economic size, measured by GDP or GDP per capita, is a simple and readily available data measure of a country's overall economic output. Trade balance, a comparison of a country's exports and imports, shows a country's role in international trade. Currency strength, analyzed by a nation's currency value, indicates economic stability and leadership. Innovation rankings, based on metrics like patent registrations, research & development spending, and venture capital activity, assess a country's innovative capacity. Global governance indicators, assessed by institutions like the World Bank, highlight the foundations for sustainable economic growth. Combining these approaches offers a different perspective, with GDP size capturing economic power, trade balance and currency strength focusing on international influence, innovation rankings, and governance indicators highlighting the underlying framework for economic success. No single method is perfect, and a more comprehensive picture of economic leadership likely requires a combination of these approaches, considering the focus on the Global South leadership context.

The analysis presented next provides best-fit linear equations from the ordinary least squares method and the R-squared values used to interpret how well the data fit the linear prediction line for several scatter plots. Each scatter plot shows the relationship between an economic factor and our leadership index. We considered four economic factors including the Gross Domestic Product (GDP) per capita (local currency unit [LCU] per international $), Gross National Income (GNI) per capita (constant LCU), Purchasing Power Parity (PPP) conversion factor, and the Gini Coefficient Index (named after statistician and sociologist Dr. Corrado Gini). Each economic metric was acquired from the World Bank 2023 Data. Before proceeding to the results, we discuss the methodology used to create the Global South Leadership (GSL) Index.

Methodology: The Global South Leadership Index

The newly developed instrument, the GSL Index framework, includes thirteen indices that score and rank fourteen countries representing four distinct regions. (Please see Appendix 1 for an inclusive table). It was developed by combining the ratings of each of the thirteen indices and averaging all indices' scores by country. To create the GSL Index and to make comparisons or determine if trends exist between countries, scores were recorded for each index for the fourteen countries. Most indices are based on a 0 to 100 percent scale, with zero indicating the worst and 100 indicating the best. However, some of these indices have different lower and upper points, which could contribute differently to the GSL Index if used in their original form. If indices are kept in their raw form, some will have more influence than others. Instead, the desired approach is to have a balanced index with equal weight.

Since not all scores are evaluated on the same rating scale, this issue of inconsistent scales was addressed by converting all scores to a 0 to 100 percent scale, with a value of 100 percent indicating the best rating score and a value of 0 percent as the worst rating score for each scale. Additionally, one of the GSL Index's rating scales was the opposite compared to all other indices, where the lower the rating, the better the outcome, and the higher the rating, the worse the outcome. To address this issue of opposite outcome scales, the original rating scales were converted on a 0 to 100 percent scale and then the score was subtracted from 100 percent. All indices prior to the conversion consisted of scoring scales with a larger value indicating a better outcome, except the Global Peace Index.

For indices with a scoring scale between 1.111 and 5.000 (Global Peace Index), where the value of 1.111 indicates the "most" peaceful country, we converted these scores based on the following formula and then multiplied the score by 100 percent.

$$\text{Adjusted Score} = 1 - \frac{(Score - 1.111)}{(5 - 1.111)} \times 100 \; percent$$

For indices that had a scoring scale between 1 percent and 100 percent (Global Marketing Potential Index – GMPI), these scores were converted based on the following formula:

$$\text{Adjusted Score} = \frac{(Score - 1)}{(100 - 1)} \times 100 \; percent$$

Once all scores per index were adjusted based on a 0 to 100 percent scale, each country was averaged across all indices to form the GSL Index. Fourteen countries were sorted and ranked based on this newly created GSL Index. The reasoning for averaging across all indices indicates that each index is equally important. Although there may be a strong indication that some indices may be more important than others, the goal was to use a plethora of indices across many economic and social metrics. By taking an average of many indices that explain the distinctive characteristics of each country, the findings yield a near-optimal index of a combination of economic and social performance.

Within the analysis, we included and examined several countries from multiple regions of the world, all part of the Global South. Two countries under consideration were removed from the final analysis due to limited information available for these two nations. The first country removed from the analysis was Taiwan. Out of the thirteen selected indices, there were no known scores for the country of Taiwan in eight out of these thirteen indices. The key data gap stems from the complex relationship between Taiwan and China. China, a major power, considers Taiwan a breakaway province, while Taiwan views itself as an independent nation. (Due to China's significant economic and political clout, many of the thirteen indices combine data from both China and Taiwan and report it as a single score for China. This approach renders Taiwan's specific data unavailable). The other country removed from the analysis was Venezuela. Venezuela has gone through periods of decline, including economic and political instability. Often instability leads to poor performance measure scores. Two of the index scores were unavailable for Venezuela, and several economic factors were unavailable, including the GDP per capita. Due to a nation's poor economic performance, leaders often conceal information from the public. Important economic metrics are unavailable because of the concealment of information. For several reasons, other countries within the analysis did not have scores for each index. It is important to disclose countries and the index whose scores are not made available. Vietnam did not have any score for the Social Progress Index (SPI). Thus, we analyze thirteen scores for each country except Vietnam, which only consists of twelve metric scores.

To understand the relationships between the GSL Index and other economic metrics, several scatter plots of each economic metric and GSL Index score were created. Economic metrics considered for the analysis included GDP per capita (see Figure 1), PPP (see Figure 2), Gini Coefficient Index (see Figure 3), and GNI per capita (see Figure 4). Once the scatter plots were created, noticeable characteristics within each chart were observed.

Subsets of the thirteen indices were generated to see whether the proposed technique of weighting all indices equally was adequate. The first subset of indices includes nine of the original thirteen indices (Global Innovation Index, Global Sustainable Competitiveness Index, Global Economic Freedom Index, Global Marketing Potential Index, Global Human Development Index, Global Peace Index, Global Education Index, Global Environmental Performance Index, and the Global Transparency Index) (see Appendices 2, 4, 6, and 8). The second subset of indices includes six of the thirteen indices (Global Human Development Index, Global Happiness Index, Global Education Index, Global Health Security Index, Social Progress Index, and Global Gender Gap Index) (see Appendices 3, 5, 7, and 9). The next step was to conduct the same analysis by averaging across all six indices for subset one and nine indices for the second subset. These subset indices were plotted for each economic metric using the updated GSL Index score. (see scatter plots in Appendices 2 through 9).

We notice distinctive patterns between all sets of indices between the scatter plots for each respective economic metric, indicating that the approach of using thirteen indices is appropriate. All GDP per capita versus the GSL Index scatter plots show a fairly large R-squared value, indicating a fairly strong relationship between GDP per capita and the GSL Index score.

Drawing comparisons between countries for various metrics can be a valuable exercise, but it is important to acknowledge the limitations of data availability and comparability. Take, for instance, the cases of Taiwan and Venezuela. Due to its unique political status, some international organizations do not include Taiwan in their datasets. This can create gaps in information and make direct comparisons with other countries challenging. Political and economic turmoil in Venezuela can lead to inconsistencies or unreliability in data collection and reporting.

We sourced the GDP per capita, the PPP conversion factor, GDP (LCU per international $), and GNI per capita (constant LCU) from the World Bank for 2023. We wanted to determine the relationships between the GSL Index and each of these economic factors by creating several scatter plots. Multiple versions of combinations of indices formed the GSL Index. The first developed GSL Index included all indices (see Appendix 1). The other developed GSL indices used nine or six indices (see Appendices 2 and 3). The results of the scatterplots presented comparable and, in some instances, identical perspectives or representations of the data. The findings provided support for the methodology used.

All charts examining the relationship between the Gini Coefficient Index, GNI per capita, and PPP and the GSL Index or subsets of leadership indices yielded low R-squared values, indicating a poor linear fit, while all charts examining the relationship between the GDP per capita and the GSL Index or subsets of leadership indices yielded high or moderately high R-squared values. Although a high R-squared value is usually most desirable, a low R-squared helps identify certain countries that may be extremely unordinary in an economic metric compared to other comparable nations; otherwise known as the influence of outliers. In particular, when examining the GNI per capita and PPP charts, the countries of Vietnam, Indonesia, and, to some extent, Chile have a large GNI per capita and PPP value compared to the other countries analyzed in this Element.

GNI per capita represents the ratio between the GNI and the midyear population. GNI is the sum of value added by all resident producers plus any product taxes (less subsidies) not included in the valuation of output plus net receipts of primary income (compensation of employees and property income) from abroad and is represented by each country's respective currency. PPP conversion factor represents the number of units of a country's currency required to buy the same amounts of goods and services in the domestic market as the U.S. dollar would buy in the United States. A country with a large PPP conversion factor and a large GNI per capita with respect to each of the countries' currencies indicates a weakened currency compared to the U.S. dollar. Both Vietnam and Indonesia have extremely high PPP and GNI per capita values compared to other countries in the analysis, indicating that both of these countries have very weak currencies compared to the U.S. dollar. A common reason for Vietnam's and Indonesia's depreciated currency is that Vietnam and Indonesia have large trade deficits mainly due to their reliance on importing more goods and raw materials compared to the country's level of exports (GNI per capita [constant LCU] by country; Vietnam – PPP conversion factor; United States – Gini Coefficient Index).

Also, the Gini Coefficient Index measures the extent to which the distribution of income (or, in some cases, consumption expenditure) among individuals or households within an economy deviates from a perfectly equal distribution. A Gini Coefficient Index of 0 represents perfect equality, while an index of 100 implies perfect inequality. Even though there may not necessarily be any outliers for the Gini Coefficient Index, as the values must all be within the range of 0 to 100, a low R-squared reflects the complexity of the relationship between the Gini Coefficient Index and the GSL Index. Instead, the charts with the Gini Coefficient Index may help identify patterns about which regions have countries with consistent equitable economic performance. We can observe from the Gini Coefficient Index charts that Asian countries consistently fall remarkably close to one another, while African countries are quite distant with respect to their Gini Coefficient value.

The GDP per capita charts show large R-squared values, indicating that there is a strong positive linear relationship between GDP per capita and the GSL Index or any subset of indices. This indicates that the GSL Index performs similarly to the GDP per capita. Many of the indices used to create the GSL Index are economic measures that are affected by countries' GDP per capita, but the difference concerns how the GSL Index considers multiple other metrics that GDP per capita does not include such as health, social, and equitable measures. Hence, a large variability of GDP per capita is explained solely by the GSL Index, and the variability of GDP per capita is explained by other metrics.

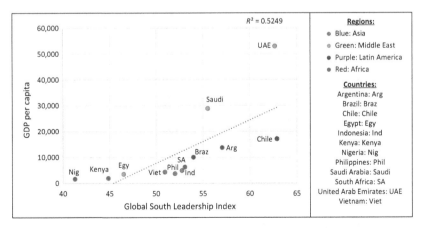

Figure 1 GSL Index and GDP per capita.
This figure was created by the authors based on information from Appendix 1 and World Bank DataBank.

GDP and GSL Index

The critical implications drawn from the GDP per capita and GSL Index scatter-plot are not to be overlooked. They can have a significant impact on the analysis and decision-making process. The most critical criteria are the outliers. Middle Eastern countries such as UAE and Saudi Arabia have an exceptionally large GDP per capita in correspondence with the GSL Index measure. In contrast, South American countries, including Chile and Argentina have smaller GDP per capita in relation to the developed GSL Index measure. Another noticeable characteristic of Figure 1 is that we can draw a "cone" shape with the countries. The cone shape indicates that countries that receive a lower GSL Index score from the developed methodology are relatively similar in GDP per capita, whereas countries with a higher GSL Index score have a wide dispersion of GDP per capita.

An explanation for this relationship could yield from the governance dynamics and economic policies within countries. Nations with lower GSL Index scores may exhibit more centralized or authoritarian governance structures, where economic opportunities and resources are often concentrated among a select few. This can result in a relatively uniform distribution of GDP per capita, as wealth tends to be controlled by a small elite. At the same time, most of the population experiences similar levels of economic well-being or deprivation. On the other hand, countries with higher GSL Index scores may embrace more decentralized or democratic governance models, fostering a broader spectrum of economic outcomes. Policies promoting entrepreneurship, innovation, and investment in such environments may lead to a wider dispersion of GDP per capita. While some regions or sectors may experience rapid economic growth and prosperity, others may lag due to factors such as infrastructure deficiencies, institutional weaknesses, or socioeconomic disparities.

Furthermore, the relationship between GSL Index scores and GDP per capita dispersion may also reflect the effectiveness of governance in fostering inclusive growth. Nations with strong leadership and effective institutions may be better equipped to implement policies that promote equitable economic development, thereby reducing disparities in income and wealth among their citizens. Conversely, weak or ineffective governance structures may exacerbate inequalities, leading to a wider gap between society's wealthiest and poorest segments. Thus, the relationship between GSL Index scores and the dispersion of GDP per capita underscores the complex interplay between governance, economic policy, and socioeconomic outcomes within countries. Understanding these dynamics is crucial for policymakers and analysts seeking to address issues of inequality and promote sustainable development on both national and global scales.

Another important note is that the scatterplot of all the indices and six indices' charts showing the relationship between GDP per capita and the GSL Index are remarkably similar, indicating that the method of using an average across the indices is an appropriate method to create the GSL Index. There is very little change between each point, showing consistency between six and thirteen indices. South American countries tend to have higher leadership metric scores and lower GDP per capita, while Middle Eastern countries tend to have higher leadership metric scores and higher GDP per capita. The other countries representing African and Asian regions have lower leadership scores and lower GDP per capita, once again supporting the finding that as countries yield lower leadership scores, their GDP per capita is consistently lower. Hence, we show there is a cluster of points within the chart. The six indices we selected are ones that we believe are highly influential on a country's performance.

UAE and Saudi Arabia GDP Outliers

The high GDP per capita of the UAE and Saudi Arabia within the Global South are primarily driven by their vast oil reserves, strategic locations, and initiative-taking economic diversification efforts. However, this economic prosperity comes with challenges related to income inequality and dependence on a finite resource. The high GDP per capita of the UAE and Saudi Arabia compared to other countries in the Global South can be attributed to a confluence of factors: The UAE and Saudi Arabia possess vast oil and natural gas reserves. This has been a primary driver of their economic growth, generating significant export revenue and fueling rapid development. Furthermore, the UAE and Saudi Arabia benefit from their strategic location in the Persian Gulf, which serves as a crucial energy passage and grants them close access to significant customers and well-established commercial channels. By strategically placing themselves, they are able to efficiently use their resources and attract international investment.

While oil and gas remain crucial, both countries have recognized the need for economic diversification. The UAE has established itself as a financial center, a hub for tourism and logistics, and is investing heavily in renewable energy. Both Saudi Arabia and the UAE have embarked on ambitious national transformation plans known as Abu Dhabi Economic Vision 2030. These initiatives go beyond mere economic diversification and represent a significant shift in leadership style. These visions represent comprehensive roadmaps to foster sustainable development, economic diversification, and societal advancement.

Saudi Arabia's Vision 2030, launched in 2016, serves as a blueprint for transitioning the kingdom's economy away from its heavy reliance on oil revenue toward a more diversified, knowledge-based economy. Central to this vision is promoting private sector growth, investment in human capital development, and enhancing non-oil sectors such as tourism, entertainment, and technology. Through initiatives like NEOM, the Red Sea Project, and the development of a vibrant cultural sector, Saudi Arabia aims to create new opportunities for employment, entrepreneurship, and innovation while fostering a more open and dynamic society. Similarly, the UAE's Abu Dhabi Economic Vision 2030, launched in 2021, underscores the nation's commitment to building a competitive and knowledge-based economy driven by innovation, sustainability, and social cohesion. Emphasizing the principles of economic diversification, technological advancement, and environmental stewardship, the UAE seeks to position itself as a global hub for innovation, entrepreneurship, and sustainable development. Initiatives such as the Mars Mission, the Abu Dhabi Economic Vision 2030, and the Dubai Clean Energy Strategy exemplify the UAE's initiative-taking approach toward embracing emerging technologies, fostering talent, and mitigating environmental challenges.

The pursuit of Abu Dhabi Economic Vision 2030 reflects a departure from traditional leadership models characterized by dependency on oil revenue and centralized decision-making toward more inclusive, forward-thinking approaches. Both Saudi Arabia and the UAE have demonstrated a willingness to embrace innovation, empower their citizens, and engage with global partners to drive sustainable growth and prosperity. These visions signal a shift toward collaborative leadership, whereby governments, private sector entities, and civil society work hand in hand to achieve common goals. By fostering partnerships with international corporations, academic institutions, and technology pioneers, Saudi Arabia and the UAE seek to leverage global expertise and resources to accelerate their economic transformation. Additionally, Abu Dhabi Economic Vision 2030 is committed to empowering youth and women as catalysts for change and progress. Through investments in education, training, and entrepreneurship, both nations aim to unlock the full potential of their human capital and create a more inclusive and diversified workforce. Furthermore, these visions reflect a long-term strategic outlook emphasizing resilience, adaptability, and future readiness. By investing in renewable energy, innovative technology, and innovation sectors, Saudi Arabia and the UAE are positioning themselves to thrive in a rapidly evolving global landscape characterized by disruptive technologies, climate change, and geopolitical shifts.

Both the UAE and Saudi Arabia have used their oil wealth to invest heavily in infrastructure development, creating modern transportation networks, logistics facilities, and special economic zones. Additionally, both countries have established sizeable sovereign wealth funds, essentially state-owned investment funds fueled by oil revenue. These funds invest in domestic infrastructure projects and international ventures.

Foreign investment has become a cornerstone of Saudi Arabia's economic diversification strategy. Saudi Arabia's economic diversification strategy is based on foreign investment, akin to a new leadership model. This strategy strategically attracts capital and expertise, fostering the growth of a dynamic and diverse industrial landscape, demonstrating a new leadership type. Saudi Arabia's Vision 2030 aims to reduce its dependence on oil and build a robust, knowledge-based economy. Foreign investment plays a crucial role in achieving this vision, with Saudi Arabia attracting significant investments in key infrastructure sectors like transportation, energy, and telecommunications. This influx of foreign capital has facilitated the development of diverse industries beyond oil and gas, such as automotive and aerospace. Investments in high-speed internet and data centers are paving the way for a flourishing tech industry. A futuristic mega-city project, NEOM represents a bold leadership vision spearheaded by Crown Prince Mohammed bin Salman. The name "NEOM" is a combination of Ancient Greek prefix "NEO" signifying "new" and 'M' indicating Mostaqbal, an Arabic term denoting "future." Given that many people believe the project is too ambitious, there is a chance that it will never be completely executed. The project aims to build a city from the ground up, nestled amidst the breathtaking landscapes of northwest Saudi Arabia, focusing on sustainability, technological integration, and a thriving knowledge-based economy. The city will be powered by 100 percent renewable energy, with plans for a futuristic transportation system using autonomous vehicles and high-speed rail.

With a strong focus on prioritizing a superior standard of living, NEOM is focused on providing top-tier educational, healthcare, and recreational amenities. Despite facing challenges like attracting talent and navigating complex logistics, it represents a paradigm shift for Saudi Arabia. The success of NEOM will not only transform Saudi Arabia's industrial landscape but potentially set a precedent for sustainable and technologically advanced urban development on a global scale.

It is important to note that a high GDP per capita only sometimes translates to widespread prosperity. Both countries, the UAE and Saudi Arabia, grapple with income inequality, with a sizable portion of the wealth concentrated in the hands of a small elite. Their economies are still heavily reliant on oil, making them less resilient and vulnerable to fluctuations in global oil prices.

As the UAE and Saudi Arabia's exceptional GDP per capita within the Global South are primarily driven by their vast oil and gas reserves, strategic location, and proactive efforts toward economic diversification, their reliance on natural resources and the need to address income inequality remain ongoing challenges. As outliers in the Global South due to their rich natural resources, strategic location, business-friendly policies, and government investment, they face the challenge of diversifying their economies and ensuring equitable distribution of wealth. Their experiences offer valuable insights for other developing nations seeking to accelerate economic growth and achieve sustainable development.

South America GDP Per Capita Outliers

In regards to South America, countries in this region have a high GSL Index and a low GDP per capita. While the region boasts a high GSL Index, signifying strong leadership qualities, its GDP per capita remains relatively low. This might be because the leadership prioritizes social stability and long-term economic development through investments in education and infrastructure. Additionally, external factors like a global recession could be affecting the region's economic performance. This means that South America falls below a line where GDP per capita is lower on a scatter plot with the GSL Index on the vertical axis and GDP per capita on the horizontal axis. In contrast, countries like Saudi Arabia and the UAE sit comfortably above this line, enjoying both a high GSL Index and a high GDP per capita.

The data becomes more dispersed as we move further up the GSL Index scale (higher leadership). This suggests that high-performing leadership styles vary more significantly than low-performing ones. Conversely, countries on the lower end of the GSL Index spectrum tend to be consistently clustered together, indicating a need for more differentiation in their leadership approaches. Interestingly, for countries with a high GSL Index, there is a much wider spread in terms of GDP per capita. This implies that strong leadership only sometimes guarantees a high GDP per capita. Other factors like resource allocation, infrastructure, or economic policies might influence a country's economic success.

Brazil, Chile, and Argentina have higher GDP per capita than many African and Asian countries due to a combination of historical factors, institutional differences, and economic strategies. Historically, these South American countries benefited from European colonization, which transferred knowledge, technology, and institutions that laid the groundwork for economic development. These countries also possess valuable natural resources, such as agricultural land, minerals, and oil reserves, which generate significant income and fuel economic growth through resource exports.

South America's leadership landscape has been shaped by various leadership styles, from authoritarian dictatorships to charismatic leaders who championed social change. Former leaders, often charismatic and populist, built strong followings based on promises of social justice and economic prosperity. However, the tensions between authoritarian control and inspirational change continue to play out in contemporary South America. The historical focus on obedience may sometimes result in a dearth of entrepreneurial spirit, a prevalent rentier model (characterized by seeking rents and a landlord mindset), or a deep unwillingness to question the existing state of affairs. At the same time, the need for transformative leadership can contribute to dissatisfaction with democratic processes. To move forward, South America must learn from its past leadership styles and strive instead for a future-oriented leadership, a different style of leadership, where leaders empower citizens, foster participation, and prioritize long-term development over short-term charisma. This requires nurturing strong democratic institutions, promoting open dialogue, and encouraging critical thinking. By fostering a culture of responsible leadership and active citizenship, South America can move beyond the shadows of its past and forge a future built on collaboration and shared prosperity.

Institutionally, Brazil, Chile, and Argentina have generally had more stable governments compared to many African and Asian nations. The current new stability, if properly managed/implemented, might foster an environment conducive to long-term economic planning and investment. Additionally, these countries need to increase their investment in infrastructure development, such as transportation networks, communication systems, and energy grids, which facilitate trade, the movement of goods and people, and economic activity.

Economically, Brazil, Chile, and Argentina have undergone periods of industrialization, diversifying their economies beyond resource extraction and fostering domestic manufacturing. They have also embraced trade liberalization policies, opening their economies to international trade and foreign investment, boosting exports, technology access, and overall economic activity.

However, it is important to recognize that while having a greater GDP per capita, these countries still have significant economic inequality and their economies are susceptible to changes in global commodity prices. South American countries enjoy some advantages, yet they also face enduring hurdles. Undoubtedly, their GDP per capita is low when compared to that of developed nations. The phenomenon of economic development is intricate, and this is part of the growing pains.

If we consider the GSL Index as a test that measures leadership effectiveness, the GDP per capita stays constant (the vertical axis does not change), while the GSL Index scores vary (the horizontal axis changes). This means that countries are primarily affected horizontally based on their leadership performance rather than vertically in terms of economic output. We will likely see a more complex picture if we factor in GDP per capita changes (vertical movement). Countries with consistently high performance across various indices (beyond just the GSL Index) would likely diverge even more significantly, indicating their exceptional leadership across multiple aspects. For example, consider Chile and Argentina. While these two countries might be geographically close, their GSL Index scores could place them further apart on the scatter plot, suggesting Chile demonstrates stronger leadership qualities across various dimensions than Argentina. Additionally, both might outperform other South American countries in terms of the GSL Index, even though their GDP per capita might differ.

As a result, this approach emphasizes the complicated relationship between leadership and economic progress. While strong leadership is essential, it is just one piece of the puzzle. Effective policies and resource management also play a crucial role in driving a country's economic success. The methodology and analysis presented in the Element demonstrate that leadership and economic wealth are not necessarily linked, and strong leadership can exist even in countries with lower GDP per capita. Furthermore, the GSL Index allows for isolating the impact of leadership on a country's position, while some countries consistently outperform others in leadership metrics.

Nigeria GDP Outlier

Nigeria is unique in Africa's economic scene, characterized by a high GDP per capita. However, it is difficult to translate this GDP per capita growth into widespread prosperity for its population. Nigeria experiences impressive economic growth due to its abundant natural resources, specifically oil and gas, which contribute to its wealth. Nigeria's GDP per capita has been greatly enhanced by its abundant natural resources, propelling it to become the largest economy in Africa based on nominal GDP per capita (World Bank, 2024).

Nigeria is facing major challenges related to economic leadership. First, there is a vast inequality in wealth distribution. Despite the abundance of oil wealth, prosperity has not been evenly distributed. A considerable number of individuals in Nigeria struggle to meet the national poverty line. Secondly, income inequality is a significant challenge encountered by numerous resource-rich countries. Additionally, infrastructure plays a crucial role in nations' economic development. Additionally, Nigeria's infrastructure poses significant challenges in key sectors such as transportation and power generation. The lack of economic diversification and development in non-oil sectors is a significant obstacle to Nigeria's progress.

While corruption remains a major obstacle that cannot be overlooked, Nigeria's ranking on Transparency International's Corruption Perception Index has consistently been low, which has a negative impact on foreign investment and poses obstacles to economic growth. As a result, the Nigerian government has come to acknowledge the drawbacks of depending solely on oil and is taking steps to broaden the country's economic base and the importance of sectors such as agriculture, manufacturing, and information technology.

Another aspect that should not be neglected is that Nigeria's population is experiencing rapid growth from 229.2 million in 2024 to 377 million by 2050 (IMF, 2024) which creates a range of challenges and opportunities. The situation in Nigeria results in a significant expansion of the labor force, which in turn puts a strain on resources and adds pressure to social services. The ability to successfully diversify the economy will play a crucial role in absorbing the expanding workforce.

Nigeria's economy is expected to grow by 3.1% in 2024, reflecting its robust economic performance (IMF), and can be largely attributed to its abundant natural resources and leadership approach. Nevertheless, Nigeria faces obstacles such as income inequality, infrastructure limitations, and corruption that impede its ability to transform wealth into broad-based economic development.

Therefore, Nigeria, Africa's largest economy and most populous country has the potential to become an economic leader in Africa and the Global South. However, achieving this requires addressing major issues and implementing significant changes. Key strategies in addition to a more powerful, forward-thinking leadership role, include economic restructuring and diversification, infrastructure development, human capital investment, and regional integration.

Additionally, Nigeria's economy is sensitive to oil price fluctuations, making diversification beyond oil essential. The government should promote development in non-oil industries like agriculture, manufacturing, and information technology to create employment, promote innovation, and provide long-term income streams. Investing in dependable infrastructure, such as power grids, transportation networks, and communication systems, can lower manufacturing costs, boost commerce, and attract international investment. Public–private partnerships can finance these projects.

Also, investing in human capital is essential for a prosperous economy in Nigeria. Nigeria should emphasize excellence in education at all levels and invest in healthcare to increase the well-being of its people. The African Continental Free Trade Area (AfCFTA) entered into force in May 2019, offers Nigeria a unique opportunity to broaden its regional economic footprint. Likewise, addressing security concerns is crucial for fostering economic progress.

Nigeria has significant prospects for economic progress due to the digital revolution. By investing in digital infrastructure, promoting tech entrepreneurship, and fostering an inventive culture, Nigeria may effectively allocate resources to develop its human capital, which is crucial for a thriving economy.

PPP and GSL Index

The PPP Index compares the cost of living between different countries. It aims to show how much a basket of goods would cost in various locations. However, specific implications and outcomes must be considered when interpreting the PPP Index.

One implication is that high-income inequality within a country can lead to PPP Index outliers. For example, a country with significant income disparity may have a high average income, but most of the population may not enjoy that standard of living. This can make the PPP seem higher than the actual living experience for most people. An example is the UAE, where a large skilled expatriate workforce earns high salaries, but the unskilled foreign workers have a different income level.

Another implication is that the PPP Index may only capture some essential expenses. For instance, the PPP Index may only partially reflect costs such as housing or healthcare significantly higher than average in a particular country. This can lead to underestimating the genuine cost of living in a country, particularly for those expenses not fully captured by the PPP Index. For example, the PPP calculation may not adequately account for housing and healthcare costs, which can vary widely from one location to another. As a result, individuals or households in areas with disproportionately high expenses for these necessities may find their purchasing power diminished relative to what the PPP suggests. This discrepancy can exacerbate income inequality by disproportionately affecting lower-income groups who must allocate a larger portion of their earnings toward these essential but unaccounted-for expenses. Furthermore, underestimating the actual cost of living can distort economic analyses and policy decisions, potentially leading to inadequate resource allocation or ineffective interventions addressing socioeconomic disparities.

Figure 2 GSL Index and PPP.

This figure was created by the authors based on information from Appendix 1 and World Bank DataBank.

The data for PPP is based on a logarithmic scale to empathize with the results. For some countries, the PPP values are exceptionally large in magnitude compared to other countries, which have values of less magnitude for certain metrics.

Vietnam and Indonesia PPP Outliers

Vietnam and Indonesia are outliers in the PPP Index within the South America region of the Global South. These include rapid economic growth, a young and growing workforce population, a focus on manufacturing, and strategic government policies. Both countries have experienced significant economic growth. Indonesia's gross domestic product growth is forecast to average 5.1 percent per year from 2024 to 2026, and Vietnam's economic growth is accelerating and could meet or exceed the government's 6.5 percent target this year, according to Planning and Investment Minister Nguyen Chi Dung (World Bank, 2024). The rise in GDP per capita in these two Asian nations leads to an upsurge in earnings and consumer expenditure. The growth of the young labor force, as said, is a key component that contributes to the rise of economic productivity and an increased ability for production and consumption. Consequently, Vietnam and Indonesia have become major manufacturing hubs, attracting foreign investment and generating exports.

The presence of a strategic leadership vision had a significant impact on both of these nations. The implementation of strategic government policies, which focus on boosting foreign direct investment, infrastructure development, and export-oriented sectors, has been essential in driving economic growth. However, it is important to acknowledge income inequality and regional variations within these countries. Additionally, a comparison with other developing nations reveals the role of factors like resource dependence and political stability in shaping overall purchasing power. Vietnam and Indonesia's diversified economies and relative political stability have contributed to their outlier status in the PPP Index within the Global South.

Chile and UAE PPP Outliers

Due to several factors, Chile and the UAE may be outliers in the PPP Index. In the case of Chile, high-income inequality and a high cost of living in major cities, such as Santiago, contribute to the deviation from the expected correlation between income and cost of living. In the UAE, a large expatriate population earning high salaries and the high cost of non-tradable goods, such as transportation and utilities, contribute to the outlier status compared to other countries. The high cost of non-tradable goods and services, such as transportation or utilities in the UAE, can also contribute to the outlier status. Government subsidies on essential goods can artificially lower the cost of living as measured by the PPP, making the countries appear cheaper than their typical market value. Further research can include analyzing the Gini Coefficient Index to measure income inequality, examining cost of living reports specific to major cities, and evaluating the composition of the PPP basket, and how it may not capture certain local realities.

Nigeria PPP Outlier

Nigeria is a notable exception in the developing world when it comes to PPP and its role in the global economy, and we can observe significant differences in PPP and uneven development. Nigeria has a significant advantage in terms of PPP, which indicates that its citizens can obtain more value for their money than developed nations. The reason behind this is the presence of a sizable number of young population and a comparatively affordable cost of living (World Bank, 2023). However, the benefits of PPP programs have not translated into widespread prosperity or equitable distribution of wealth. The disparity in income levels is striking, as a considerable segment of the population resides below the poverty threshold. Nigeria's economy has shown varied performance due to its heavy reliance on oil exports and the unpredictable fluctuations in oil prices. Despite attempts to diversify the economy, consistent outcomes have not been achieved, which may indicate they need a more strategically oriented leadership type vision.

Urbanization has become a pressing issue as cities continue to grow at an alarming rate, (for example, Lagos is one of the largest and fastest growing mega-cities in Africa at nearing 16 million: population's annual average growth rate is 3.2 percent, above the national growth rate of 2.6 percent, and projected to become the world's most populous city by 2100, with 88.3 million) (World Bank, 2023), placing immense strain on resources and exacerbating the already significant wealth disparity between different socioeconomic groups. The inadequate state of transportation and power grids hinders business operations and hampers productivity, and security issues have a significant impact (Qureshi, 2023).

Through strategic measures and leveraging its unique advantages, Nigeria could emerge as a prominent economic powerhouse in the Global South; nevertheless, moving ahead necessitates bold leadership, consistent dedication, and the implementation of well-thought-out policies to achieve sustainable growth. It is important to prioritize the development of non-oil sectors such as agriculture, manufacturing, and services. Additionally, investing in infrastructure upgrades can enhance connectivity and stimulate investment. Establishing stability is also crucial for attracting investment and promoting economic activity.

Gini Coefficient and GSL Index

The Gini Coefficient Index is a measure of income inequality within a population. It quantifies the extent to which the distribution of income or wealth among individuals or households within an economy deviates from a perfectly equal distribution. The coefficient is represented by a number between 0 and 1, where 0 represents perfect equality (everyone has the same income) and one represents perfect inequality (one person has all the income, while everyone else has none).

The Gini Coefficient is calculated based on income or wealth data from a population, and it does not directly measure GDP per capita or PPP. However, it is often used alongside these economic indicators to provide insights into a country's wealth or income distribution. A higher Gini Coefficient Index suggests greater income inequality, which can have social and economic implications for a society.

There could be several reasons why Nigeria, Chile, UAE, South Africa, and Brazil might be outliers in terms of the Gini Coefficient Index. In the case of Nigeria, the high Gini coefficient is attributed to factors such as corruption, unequal access to resources, regional disparities in development, and dependence on oil revenue. This has resulted in a large gap between the rich and the poor, with a small percentage of the population controlling a significant share of the wealth. In Chile, the high Gini coefficient may result from factors such as the privatization of social services, the historical legacy of dictatorship,

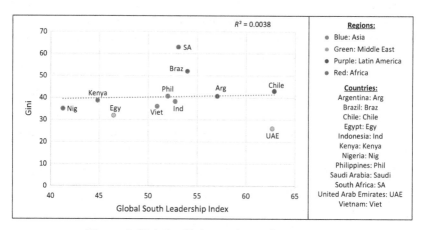

Figure 3 Gini Coefficient Index and GSL Index.
This figure was created by the authors based on information from Appendix 1 and World
Bank DataBank.

and neoliberal economic policies. This has led to unequal access to quality
services based on socioeconomic status and entrenched disparities in wealth and
opportunity. The UAE's Gini coefficient reflects the substantial income disparities between the local Emirati population and the large expatriate workforce.
The country's reliance on oil revenue has led to a widening wealth gap between
citizens and noncitizens and a reliance on low-wage migrant labor. South
Africa's high Gini coefficient is a result of its history of apartheid and colonialism. Despite efforts to address inequality through policies such as Black
economic empowerment, racial disparities in wealth and access to opportunities
persist. Factors such as land ownership patterns, educational inequalities, and
structural barriers contribute to the country's high Gini coefficient.

In Brazil, historical factors such as colonialism, slavery, and land concentra-
tion have contributed to enduring socioeconomic disparities. Economic policies, limited access to education and healthcare for marginalized populations,
and urbanization have also perpetuated inequality. Land inequality and a large
informal sector workforce further contribute to Brazil's high Gini coefficient.

GNI per Capita and GSL Index

The GNI per capita Index reflects a nation's total income, considering income
earned by its residents domestically and abroad. This makes it a broader
measure of economic well-being compared to the GDP per capita, which only
focuses on economic activity within a country's borders.

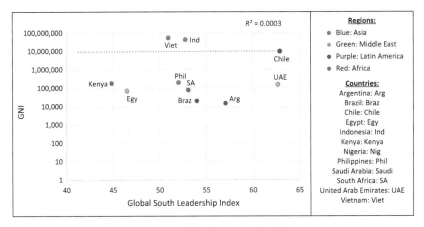

Figure 4 GSL Index and GNI.

This figure was created by the authors based on information from Appendix 1 and World Bank DataBank.

The GNI data is based on a logarithmic scale to visually comprehend the results in a comprehensive manner. For some countries, the GNI per capita values are exceptionally large compared to others, which have values of less magnitude for certain metrics.

Vietnam, Indonesia, Chile, and the UAE Are Outliers in the GNI

Vietnam and Indonesia might be outliers in the GNI per capita Index due to a combination of factors. These include economic reforms and openness, a young and skilled workforce, political stability and governance, regional differences, and strong economic growth. Both countries have implemented market-oriented reforms, focused on export-oriented manufacturing, attracted foreign direct investment, and invested in education and infrastructure. They have also enjoyed increased political stability and benefited from regional advantages in Southeast Asia. However, challenges such as income inequality, reliance on low-wage manufacturing, and sustainability concerns must be addressed over time. Despite these challenges, Vietnam and Indonesia have experienced significant economic growth and diversification, positioning themselves as regional economic powerhouses and potential leaders in the region's economic strategy.

Chile and the UAE might be outliers in the GNI per capita Index due to their resource wealth, foreign investment, financial hub status, economic diversification, and social inequality. Both countries possess significant natural resources, such as copper in Chile and oil and gas in the UAE, which generate substantial income through exports. They also attract foreign investment, which boosts their income generation. The UAE's status as a financial hub attracts international financial institutions, generating income through fees and services. Additionally, both countries have tried diversifying their economies and invested in human capital development. However, considering other indicators, such as the Human Development Index (HDI) and Gini coefficient, is important to better understand their economic well-being.

Linking Economic Leadership and Political Change in the Global South

According to S'thembile Cele (2024, January 31), the relationship between economic leadership and political leadership in the Global South is complex and constantly evolving. Challenges such as short-termism, resource dependence, and institutional weakness can hinder economic growth and development. However, strategies such as development-oriented leadership and technocratic governments can help link economic and political change.

Prominent examples of countries in the Global South recently demonstrating economic leadership alongside political change include India, Indonesia, and Chile. These countries have focused on areas such as technological innovation, infrastructure development, and social development to drive economic growth and reduce inequality. According to the World Bank (2023), India's GDP and PPP have led to economic growth. India is one of the fastest-growing economies in the world and aims to reach high-middle income status by 2047. The country has made noteworthy progress in reducing extreme poverty; although, the pace has slowed during the COVID-19 pandemic. Inequality in consumption, the weak education system, and child malnutrition remain challenges, and there are concerns about the quality of jobs and low female labor force participation.

Nevertheless, India's economic outlook is positive, with real GDP growth bouncing back strongly in fiscal year 2021–2023 after contracting due to the pandemic. Accommodative monetary and fiscal policies, vaccine coverage, and strong domestic demand have supported growth. However, there are signs of moderation, and headwinds such as rising borrowed costs and inflationary pressures may impact growth in fiscal year 2023–2024. The government has been working on fiscal consolidation, with the fiscal deficit and public debt gradually declining. Revenues have increased, and pandemic-related stimulus measures have been withdrawn. The government remains committed to increasing capital spending, particularly on infrastructure, to boost growth and competitiveness. The World Bank has been working with the Indian government to enhance policies, institutions, and investments in order to promote environmentally sustainable, resilient, and inclusive development. The objective is to attain a state of high financial prosperity while simultaneously tackling the issue of climate change and diminishing economic inequalities.

Indonesia has experienced impressive economic growth and has become the tenth largest economy in terms of PPP. The country has significantly reduced poverty and is implementing a twenty-year development plan to further strengthen its economy. Indonesia has also demonstrated its leadership in international forums such as the G20 and ASEAN and has regained its upper-middle income status after the impact of the COVID-19 pandemic. The country has also made progress in addressing climate change, with support from the World Bank (World Bank, 2023).

Chile's GDP per capita and PPP have significantly impacted its economic growth. The country's sound macroeconomic policies have helped it recover from imbalances caused by the COVID-19 pandemic, such as high deficits and inflation. Fiscal and monetary tightening measures have stabilized the economy, although they have also slowed down growth in 2023. Chile aims to achieve faster, greener, and more inclusive growth. To accomplish this, the country must focus on reforms targeting productivity, technology, competition, and human capital development. These reforms are crucial for driving economic growth and ensuring that they benefit all segments of society. Inflation has been brought under control through determined monetary tightening and a decrease in supply shocks. The inflation rate closed at 3.9 percent year-on-year in 2023.

Looking ahead, Chile's economic activity is expected to gradually recover toward a trend of GDP growth of 2.0 percent in 2024. With controlled inflation and modest economic growth, poverty is projected to decrease to 5.0 percent in 2024 and remain around this level in the medium term. The Gini coefficient is projected to remain at 0.43. Chile's key challenge is moving toward higher and more inclusive growth. Growth averaged just 2 percent in the six years preceding the pandemic. Targeted reforms to address specific bottlenecks are needed to boost productivity growth, which has been declining for decades. This includes reducing regulatory barriers, fostering technology adoption, promoting competition, enhancing managerial capabilities, and increasing female labor force participation and job quality. Chile is also expected to leverage the global green transition, with both renewable energy and the plan to expand lithium production through public–private partnerships, potentially contributing to increased growth in the future (World Bank, 2023).

Saudi Arabia is undergoing a major economic transformation outlined in its Vision 2030, which aims to diversify the economy away from oil and improve the social contract. The country is shifting toward a new economic model focused on increased productivity and private sector-led growth. This transition involves improving human capital, creating a favorable business environment, enhancing public administration, and developing a flexible labor market. Saudi Arabia has signed a Technical Cooperation Program (TCP) agreement with the World Bank to support its development agenda and implement Vision 2030. The TCP covers various sectors, including investment climate, education, health, labor markets, transport, energy, urban planning, and more. The country has also become a key development partner to the World Bank, pledging significant funds to support efforts to end extreme poverty and promote shared prosperity globally (World Bank, 2023).

Leadership has a significant role in determining the level of success. The substantial growth of economic leadership has a profound influence on global geopolitics, as well as several other socioeconomic domains and emerging trends in the Global South. It challenges the traditional dominance of developed nations in global institutions and trade agreements, and developing countries, such as the BRICS-Plus bloc, are increasingly cooperating with each other on economic and political issues. Additionally, the Global South's leadership is crucial in shaping global climate policy, as climate change disproportionately impacts these countries.

The Culture of Leadership in the Global South

Leadership, the art of guiding and inspiring others toward a shared goal, manifests differently across cultures. Understanding these nuances is especially crucial in the Global South, a diverse region encompassing developing countries with unique historical and social contexts. In order to examine the idea of implicit leadership theories (ILTs) and the impact of leadership qualities and characteristics on leadership styles in the Global South, we used the Global Leadership and Organizational Behavior Effectiveness (GLOBE) project.

ILTs are an individuals' mental models of effective leadership (Eden & Leviathan, 1978). These unconscious beliefs, shaped by individual experiences and cultural norms, guide our perceptions of leaders and their behaviors. For example, someone raised in a hierarchical society might have an ILT emphasizing decisiveness and control as key leadership traits, while someone from a more collaborative culture might value consensus-building and shared decision-making.

The Global South encompasses a vast array of cultures, each with its own set of values and traditions. These cultural influences significantly impact ILTs within the region. For instance, societies that strongly emphasize collectivism, often found in the Global South, might have ILTs prioritizing leaders who value group harmony and social well-being above individual achievement (Hofstede, 1980). On the other hand, cultures with a more individualistic orientation might have ILTs that favor assertive leaders who demonstrate an intense sense of ambition. Understanding these cultural influences on ILTs allows us to identify leadership traits that resonate in the Global South.

- *Relationship building.* Leaders who prioritize building strong relationships with their followers and fostering a sense of community are likely to be perceived more favorably in many Global South cultures (House et al., 2004). This emphasis on social connection stems from the collectivist values prevalent in many parts of the region.
- *Transformational leadership.* Leaders who inspire their followers by appealing to their higher values and motivating them to achieve beyond their perceived capabilities are highly valued (Bass & Avolio, 1994). This resonates with the aspirations for progress and development, often a driving force in the Global South.
- *Cultural sensitivity.* Effective leaders in the Global South understand the importance of cultural sensitivity. They can navigate diverse cultural norms and adapt their leadership styles, accordingly, fostering trust and collaboration with a heterogeneous workforce (Javidan et al., 2008).
- *Resilience.* The Global South faces unique challenges, from resource scarcity to political instability. Leaders who demonstrate resilience and the ability to navigate complex situations are highly valued (Avolio & Yammarino, 2013).

The information presented above is broad in nature and should not be applied to any particular person without taking into account their unique circumstances. The leadership traits valued in the Global South will vary depending on the specific context. Factors like a nation's history, level of development, and dominant religious beliefs can all influence ILTs and leadership preferences. Understanding the interplay between ILT and cultural influences allows for a more nuanced understanding of leadership in the Global South. Leaders who recognize their own ILTs and are sensitive to their followers' cultural context will be better positioned to inspire, motivate, and guide their nations toward a brighter future.

The Global Leadership and Organizational Behavior Effectiveness (GLOBE) study, is a major research program investigating the relationships between societal culture, leadership styles, and organizational practices across various cultures. Launched in the 1990s, it is considered one of the most comprehensive studies of its kind in the social sciences (House et al., 2004). Based on the GLOBE study, there is a variety of leadership styles:

- *Charismatic/value-based.* Leaders inspire with vision and strong values (common in South America and parts of Asia).

- *Participative.* Leaders involve others in decision-making (common in parts of Asia).
- *Humanitarian.* Leaders prioritize employee well-being and development (less common, but present in some regions).
- *Autocratic.* Leaders make decisions with little input from others (more typical in regions with high power distance).
- *Self-protective.* Leaders focus on security and maintaining the status quo (less common).

Clustering

- *South America.* Generally, scores high on power distance, in-group collectivism, and uncertainty avoidance. Leadership styles tend toward charismatic/value-based and, to a lesser extent, participative.
- *Asia.* Scores vary greatly. East Asia tends toward high power distance and collectivism, with charismatic and participative leadership styles. South Asia can be similar but emphasizes family and social hierarchy.
- *Africa.* Scores vary depending on the region. Sub-Saharan Africa can score high on power distance and collectivism, with leadership styles leaning toward charismatic and autocratic. North Africa might show more influence from Middle Eastern cultures.
- *Middle East.* The region generally scores high on power distance and in-group collectivism. Leadership styles tend toward charismatic and autocratic.

Appendices 10–13 elaborate on the cross-cultural leadership styles and traits in the Global South.

Outlook: Can a Leadership Philosophy from the Global South Foster Global Economic Growth?

As previously discussed in the Element, the bloc of countries from the Global South is very promising and aspires to be more prominent in world affairs. These are the factors that bring about transformation. Current postcolonial leaders are more integrationist than their predecessors because they believe they can redistribute money, prestige, and power in the global political economy. This is an attempt to recognize developing countries as complete and equal players in state society and states with specific development requirements, which the industrialized Global North's false universality all too frequently overlooks. The recognition fight supports inclusive multilateralism and "non-indifference" to development in the Global South.

Although this group lacks a formal unified leadership, China has become a considerable member with a greater influence by offering vulnerable member countries infrastructure support and financing through its ambitious Belt and Road Initiative (BRI). This has enabled China to become the leading trading partner of over 120 countries (Green, 2023). However, China's influence is limited in reach and intensity, and its conduct and political values may hinder its influence. India, the UAE, Saudi Arabia, Brazil, and South Africa are among the rising nations that have established their influence in the Global South. This emphasizes that the Global South is characterized by its dynamic and diversified attributes in relation to geography, geopolitics, history, and development, placing a high emphasis on autonomy and acknowledges the significance of considering multiple perspectives. Thus, it is a contested region that does not aspire to have a single leader (The Economist, 2024). However, we strongly posit that they are actively seeking a unique and different kind of cooperation. By embracing the distinct features of each nation in the Global South, they can use the region's collective impact to build a future that is equitable, environmentally sustainable, and accessible for all. The dynamic and rapidly changing environment of the Global South, characterized by its immense potential for economic expansion and geopolitical impact, should evoke feelings of hope and optimism among readers.

No Longer Bottom of the Pyramid

Another point of progress and a departure from the Global North-South line based on GDP per capita established by former German Chancellor Willy Brandt in 1980, C.K. Prahalad coined the phrase "Bottom of the Pyramid" (BoP), and its significance to the Global South's potential is critical (Prahalad & Hart, 1999). We argue that the massive number of low-income workers in the Global South provides an immense, untapped market potential. The narrative of people experiencing poverty as just receivers of help is now being reframed, and instead, the world needs to refer to the Global South as potential customers, producers, and economic drivers. This also is a time for companies to develop new goods and services to meet the BoP population's wants and buying power of an untapped market with massive economic and other human capital potential. However, it is important to note the BoP challenges, such as issues with affordability, accessibility, and cultural acceptance of new products and services. With its vast and expanding population, the Global South has the potential for a substantial market with a drive toward economic development. Leadership is vital in realizing and adapting this positive economic outlook, and could encourage enterprises to create inclusive business models for the mutual benefit of those enterprises and the BoP population. Businesses that regard the BoP as a market opportunity rather than a burden may help drive economic growth and development in these areas.

The Global South seems to be at the forefront of promising economic growth and social progress. This progress is not without its challenges. Hence, effective leadership is crucial and urgent in navigating these complexities as we explore in this Element. Some other examples of leadership, as well as their shortcomings, can be referenced. For instance, the leadership of Singapore's first Prime Minister, the late Lee Kuan Yew, was instrumental in the country's ascent as a global innovation hub. Similarly, under President Paul Kagame's leadership, Rwanda has made significant economic development and poverty reduction strides. The interplay between this Element's leadership approach and a country's GDP and economic growth is profound. Therefore, leadership plays a crucial role in shaping a nation's economic trajectory through various political and economic processes.

As previously discussed, the Global South is positioned to have a substantial impact on global economic leadership and international development. The Global South, including emerging and growing markets in Asia, Africa, and South America, is propelling innovation and generating new opportunities for the trade of products and services. Despite variations in levels of commitment and national limitations, these areas are promoting policies for success. Moreover, they are actively formulating plans to tackle global issues such as climate change, sustainable development, and fair economic growth. They advocate for policies prioritizing social equity, environmental sustainability, and long-term economic stability. The Global South also fosters SSC, where countries share knowledge, resources, and best practices to tackle common issues and leverage collective strengths. This collaborative approach enhances their ability to influence global economic governance and ensures their perspectives are reflected in international decision-making processes. As these countries grow, they will become strong voices and influencers in shaping the future of the global economy and driving strategic initiatives benefiting not only their regions but the world at large.

Factors such as resource abundance, growing domestic markets, and investment in infrastructure and technology are fueling the economic prospective rise of the Global South. This shift in economic power could lead to a renegotiation of global trade deals, with increased SSC and pressure on established economies to offer fairer terms. Additionally, the rise of the Global South could challenge the current U.S.-centric world order, leading to a multipolar system and demanding more excellent representation in international institutions. However, there are challenges and uncertainties, including the need for significant capital investment, political instability and corruption, and the impact of climate change. Overall, the rise of the Global South presents both opportunities and challenges for companies that should consider market diversification, building local partnerships, focusing on sustainability, investing in infrastructure, and building a strong employer brand to thrive in this economic shift.

This Element launches a new concept of leadership that encompasses policy-making, institutional quality, investment in human capital, infrastructure development, promotion of innovation and entrepreneurship, external relations and trade policies, management of economic shocks, and long-term planning and vision. Effective leadership can foster an environment conducive to economic growth, while poor leadership can hinder progress and exacerbate socioeconomic challenges. The positive impacts of robust leadership on a nation's future opportunities include the implementation of favorable economic policies, the maintenance of stability and certainty, the development of human capital, and the increase of investor confidence. Strong and effective leadership is essential for promoting economic growth. Economic expertise, vision, strategic thinking, effective decision-making, and adaptability are key qualities for leaders to drive growth and success. Such leaders can create an advantageous environment that is favorable to a broader economy by cultivating these traits. However, it is essential to consider nuances such as leadership style, the balance between short-term gains and long-term sustainability, and external factors that may influence economic growth. Leadership is one of many factors that affect a country's economic development, and its influence in the global community, while it can significantly impact GDP, is not a guaranteed recipe for success although a good starting point. The success of developing countries hinges on strong and capable leadership that instills a sense of responsibility and collective consensus among the population. This emphasizes the need for leaders who can inspire accountability and promote a culture of progress in the Global South.

Complexity and Changing Dynamics

The Element's approach aims to inspire leaders within the Global South, recognizing the complexity of the global order being defined by rising powers from the Global South. Russia, for example, located in the Northern Hemisphere, is an emerging global influencer with a complex history that challenges the established world order. Despite its high GDP, Russia still faces significant disparities in wealth distribution, classifying it as an upper-middle-income region. This uneven development reflects individuals' challenges in regions beyond traditional power centers. Russia's economic strength, evident through its military power and abundant natural resources, gives it a relative advantage over many countries in the Global South. Despite economic inequality, Russia's overall development indicators, such as the HDI, surpass those of many other regions.

These days, Russia's position is complex and cannot be easily categorized. It aims to bring together different geographical areas, presenting itself as an alternative leader for countries outside traditional power centers. Russia's future relationship with other countries depends on various factors, such as the resolution of the Ukraine conflict, its economic direction, and its ability to establish itself as an alternative to Western influence. To fully comprehend Russia's position in the global order, one must consider factors beyond mere geography, including its historical legacy, economic standing, and current political goals within the Global South. Russia's relationship with regions beyond traditional power centers is subject to change and should be closely monitored as the global situation develops.

U.S. – China and the Balance of Power

Asia is the world's most strategically important region, home to over half the population and six of the world's twenty-five largest economies. It has been a driving force in global growth, accounting for over 70 percent of the increase in global GDP over the last decade. China has contributed 31 percent to this growth. Asia also hosts 19 of the top 100 universities and 10 of the 25 countries with the most patents in 2021. To remain the most powerful country, the U.S. must tap into Asia and prevent China from dominating it (Mallick, 2024).

Chinese universities have surpassed the top ten spots in a global science ranking, largely due to a shift in data underlying rankings. The Leiden University Center for Science and Technology Studies (CWTS) group issued new university rankings that add open-data sources to the traditional curated list of elite journals. These results show that the world has turned upside down in terms of university rankings, with China's position being upended. China's rapid progress in science and technology, driven by investments in research and university strength, has alarmed the U.S. and other nations. Concerns are mounting that the U.S. may be losing its competitive advantage in the technology sector to an assertive rival, with potential implications for national security, economic standing, and global influence. The new rankings will likely raise even more alarm. Chinese researchers and their sponsoring institutions place a huge premium on publishing in international journals, even those hosted by questionable publishers. Efforts are underway to enhance quality, and government payments to researchers for articles in ranked journals are being unsettled (Wagner, 2024).

The Economist (2024) states that the U.S. focus on hindering China's scientific progress is misguided. The pursuit of scholarly and scientific advancement is a key characteristic of global power in the 21st century. Both the U.S. and China invest heavily in research and development, but the current U.S. strategy of hindering China's progress through sanctions is likely to be a self-defeating endeavor. A more nuanced approach may be necessary, considering the potential benefits of collaboration with China on mutually beneficial scholarly and scientific projects. In line with the Economist, there is a leadership style that relies on tariffs and sanctions to impede and halt a country's technological progress. However, its effectiveness is debatable. The introduction of tariffs and sanctions raises ethical concerns, albeit their effectiveness is uncertain. The Economist posits that while tariffs and sanctions may be a morally justifiable method to impede a nation's technological advancement, they may not be the most efficacious means to restrain China's scientific growth. Sanctions alone are insufficient in restraining China's scientific progress, since they may unintentionally encourage China to develop self-reliant capabilities, thus diminishing U.S. influence in the future. Collaboration on scientific research offers a compelling alternative, as joint efforts in areas like medicine, clean energy, and space exploration could lead to faster breakthroughs. International information and resource sharing has the capacity to accelerate scientific progress, perhaps resulting in the discovery of solutions to global challenges that would be beyond the capabilities of any one country. Refusing to do so may result in an accelerated competition and probable spillover into additional sectors.

Despite this approach, the U.S. must continue to pursue its own scientific innovation through increased investments in research and development. Attracting top scientific minds and fostering an environment that encourages groundbreaking ideas remain key elements in this pursuit. By reevaluating its strategy and prioritizing both domestic scholarly advancements and selective collaborations with China, the U.S. can ensure continued leadership in the global scientific arena while reaping the benefits of collaborative solutions to humanity's most pressing challenges.

The U.S. also faces challenges in maintaining global leadership due to conflicts in Israel-Gaza and Russia-Ukraine, which have led to a perception of the U.S. as a non-neutral peace broker, have strained U.S. resources and diverted focus from other global issues. China's rise, through initiatives like the BRI, is the most significant challenge to U.S. global leadership.

The old rules-based international order is no longer effective in today's complex world, with traditional alliances and institutions struggling to address contemporary challenges such as climate change, cyber threats, economic inequality, and geopolitical tensions. To maintain global stability and progress, leaders must adopt innovative approaches that go beyond outdated frameworks. The current landscape is characterized by a diverse array of state and non-state actors, each with their own interests and agendas. Effective leadership requires a nuanced understanding of regional dynamics, a willingness to engage in multilateral and unconventional diplomacy, and the ability to foster cooperative relationships across a broad spectrum of stakeholders. The Element asserts that while the old international order's remnants still exist, they are insufficient for addressing the complexities of today's world. It calls for a new leadership approach that is adaptable, inclusive, and forward-thinking, capable of steering the global community through the uncertain and rapidly evolving landscape of the 21st century.

However, core institutions such as the UN Security Council and the World Trade Organization are tied in knots due to disagreements among their members. Russia is committed to disrupting U.S.-fortified norms. China is committed to building its own alternative order. In terms of trade and industrial policy, even Washington is moving away from the core tenets of post–Cold War globalization. Regional powers such as Brazil, India, Türkiye, and the Gulf states select which partner to connect with based on the specific interest or issue at hand. Even the current high-water mark for multilateral action and support for Ukraine in its fight against Russia – remains a largely Western initiative. As the old order unravels, these overlapping blocs are competing over what will replace it. Washington needs to prioritize investment, technology, and clean energy to strengthen relationships with the Global South. To build a reservoir of goodwill, U.S. leadership must listen to diverse voices from around the world it faces internationally and embracing an agenda that is repositioning the U.S. for a changing world by focusing on its democracy and economy, rebooting alliances in Europe and Asia, and embracing an agenda that resonates with more governments and people (Rhodes, 2024).

Russia's strategic moves, while not as pervasive as China's, are strategically enhancing its presence in the Middle East and other regions. Regional powers such as Iran, Türkiye, and Saudi Arabia are also recalibrating their strategies in response to the shifting dynamics.

The Global South is undergoing considerable economic and political restructuring. As the U.S. focuses on conflicts and regional instabilities, China's investments and Russia's military partnerships are creating new alliances and dependencies. Potential outcomes may diminish the influence of the U.S. and the so-called West, increase multipolarity, and economic shifts toward the Global South. To retain its leadership role, the U.S. must adapt its strategies and strengthen its alliances, balancing immediate conflict management with long-term global engagement.

Another point of contention according to a recent analysis by the London School of Economics and Political Science (2024), the COVID-19 pandemic, tensions between the U.S. and China, and conflicts in the Middle East have raised concerns about the reliability of global supply chains and the future of globalization. A study using data from the global value chains (GVCs) Indicators database examines the evolution of globalization from 2000 to 2021, focusing on GVCs and the role of China. The study highlights the importance of measuring trade on a value-added basis, as it provides a more accurate picture of world trade compared to gross trade statistics. Value-added measurements capture the contribution of each country's producers throughout the production process, including intermediate goods traded across multiple stages.

Frayer (2024) addresses three key questions: the extent of supply chain decoupling between North America and China, the increase in globalization or "nearshoring," and the role of Free Trade Agreements (FTAs) in shaping production linkages and GVCs. The results show that there was no measurable decoupling between North America and China in terms of indirect value-added production linkages. While direct trade between the U.S. and China has decreased, indirect linkages have grown, suggesting that trade in final goods is being redirected through third-party nations. The study also finds no evidence, so far, of a significant global trend toward a strong reshoring production during the analyzed period.

In terms of FTAs, the analysis stresses their quantitative significance in explaining the expansion of indirect links across nations. The impact of FTAs on GVC linkages varies across regions and specific agreements, and FTAs should still be seen as valuable tools for strengthening bonds with trading partners in global supply chains. It also suggests that assertions of deglobalization are overstated since both direct and indirect links supporting the production of goods and services have not decreased globally. The trade in services and products continue to expand, demonstrating that globalization is still occurring. Consequently, the U.S. may want to consider and give priority to the establishment of new trade agreements with allies in Asia and Europe in order to preserve its influence in the restructuring of GVCs and contribute to their long-term prosperity.

This brings attention to the matter at hand. Although there is no clear and unified leadership within this group, China has become a highly influential member, surpassing the influence of the U.S., China strategically targets vulnerable countries in need of infrastructure support and financing. However, China's influence, both in terms of reach and intensity, and its conduct and political values, may potentially hinder its influence. Other emerging powers, such as India, the UAE, Saudi Arabia, Brazil, and South Africa, also have claims to power within the Global South (The Economist, April 8, 2024). This dynamic landscape of the Global South, with its potential for growth and influence, should inspire hope and optimism.

The Prominence of the BRICS-Plus Bloc

After the fifteenth BRICS Summit in 2023, foreign policy analysts raised concerns that the bloc may be seeking to construct an alternate world order to challenge Western-led global governance. The group has diverged from the Western-led system through initiatives such as reducing reliance on the U.S. dollar and creating new institutions. In January 2024, the group welcomed new members – emphasizing the importance of diversified global leadership and a greater plurality of ideas. No doubt, the BRICS-Plus is evolving into a strategic entity dedicated to system-wide reforms, with the NDB and the Contingent Reserve Arrangement being discussed as alternatives to Western-dominated institutions like the World Bank and the IMF. The Asian Infrastructure Investment Bank, a China-led multilateral development bank, has a track record of nearly doubled membership since its founding in 2016 (Dai, 2024).

This Element supports a new concept of leadership as a driving force for change, innovation, and inclusive economic prosperity from the bottom up and middle out. It emphasizes empowering individuals and communities at the grassroots level, fostering growth that benefits all segments of society. The bloc's strategies might include creating opportunities for marginalized and underrepresented groups, promoting equitable access to resources, and ensuring fair distribution of economic gains across different socioeconomic groups. Prioritizing education, healthcare, and social services, the bloc aims to build a resilient and inclusive economy. It also encourages local entrepreneurship, supports small and medium-sized enterprises, and fosters innovation in underserved areas. This bottom-up and middle-out approach aims to harness the potential of every member, driving economic growth from within and creating a more just and inclusive society.

With the UN Sustainable Development Goals in peril and the World Bank undergoing major reforms, BRICS-Plus has an opportunity to step up with development funding and new initiatives. BRICS-Plus members are laboratories for digital and financial inclusion and innovation with rapidly evolving digital economies. These innovations are particularly relevant in the Global South, where many people live in internet poverty and are excluded from the formal financial system. However, BRICS-Plus has yet to effectively leverage the digital development expertise of its member states. BRICS-Plus member states should harness best practices from within the bloc and align their digital innovators with the World Bank's acceleration efforts to advance inclusion among the three dozen countries seeking inspiration and new development opportunities. The BRICS-Plus is poised to persist in aligning with the existing system and advocating for specific changes when necessary (East Asia Forum, 2024).

We need to recognize the increasing importance of the BRICS-Plus bloc nations, which are gaining economic and political influence in the Global South. These economies have the potential to become the next major driver of global growth. According to the Berger report (2023), this potential originates from a number of factors. The Global South has abundant natural resources that are expected to be in high demand during the commodity supercycle from 2025 to 2030. Therefore, resource-rich countries seek to diversify their economies by developing downstream businesses beyond raw material exports. This diversity can lead to a more robust and resilient economy. Also, the transition to renewable energy may help developing economies move up the value chain and participate in higher-margin activities beyond exporting fossil fuels. However, the Berger report (2023) states that challenges must be solved before the entire Global South can fully achieve its economic potential, such as the current capital spending shortage. This lack of investment may result in a scarcity of critical commodities in the future. The Global South is becoming a significant economic and political power. While there are challenges to overcome, the area has the potential to become the next engine of global growth, particularly if it can leverage its resource richness, diversify its economies, and strategically position itself in the current energy revolution. As a result, the BRICS-Plus bloc aims to reform the current global system and create a more multipolar and democratic order, reducing the representation of Western ideas and leaders in global decision-making. Currently, the bloc relies on the Western-led global governance system. Despite being connected to the West, they also challenge it and are dedicated to challenging the global governance system. However, they are currently operating within its framework. To provide a compelling alternative to the current system, the bloc will need to demonstrate a distinctive vision for the Global South and expedite development progress.

The Global South is at the forefront of economic growth and social progress. This progress is not without its challenges, and effective leadership is crucial and urgent in navigating these complexities as we explore in this Element. The relationship between this Element's leadership style and a country's GDP and economic development is significant. Leadership can significantly shape a nation's economic trajectory through various mechanisms, whether political or economic.

A new Concept of Leadership

This new concept of leadership elaborated in this Element encompasses policy-making, institutional quality, investment in human capital, infrastructure development, promotion of innovation and entrepreneurship, external relations and trade policies, management of economic shocks, and long-term planning and vision. Effective leadership can foster an environment conducive to economic growth, while poor leadership can hinder progress and exacerbate socioeconomic challenges. The positive impacts of robust leadership on national progress include the implementation of favorable economic policies, the maintenance of stability and certainty, the development of human capital, and the increase of investor confidence. Leadership traits such as economic expertise, vision and strategy, effective decision-making, and adaptability are crucial for economic growth. However, it is essential to consider nuances such as leadership style, the balance between short-term gains and long-term sustainability, and external factors that may influence economic growth. Leadership is one of many factors that influence a country's economic development, and while it can significantly impact GDP, it is not a guaranteed recipe for success. This highlights the significance of competent leadership in the Global South, evoking a sense of accountability in our readers.

Although the significance of GDP for fostering economic growth is widely recognized, one has to also acknowledge the limitations of GDP as a measure of well-being (Dynan & Sheiner, 2018). The focus on production rather than distribution, the exclusion of nonmarket activities, and the failure to measure sustainability are some drawbacks of relying solely on GDP. Leaders in the Global South relying solely on GDP for policy decisions may overlook nuances in economic well-being. Understanding GDP's limitations can lead to more informed policymaking addressing broader welfare aspects beyond GDP. Hence, there is a need for improved measurement practices that can provide leaders with more nuanced insights into economic conditions and welfare. The implications for leadership include the potential for misguided policies, a limited view of progress, and pressure to prioritize growth at any cost. Leaders prioritizing GDP growth may enact policies that intensify inequality or environmental damage or may fail to consider social indicators such as education or healthcare. Leaders may face pressure to boost GDP at any cost, even if it means compromising other aspects of their well-being.

Conclusion

Emerging markets in the Global South encompass a diverse group of countries, historically linked by the shared experiences of colonialism and a collective desire for growth. However, the narrative is currently evolving, as outlined in this Element. The Global South is no longer content to be a follower; it is emerging as a potent force for global leadership, driven by an unwavering commitment to a more equitable and sustainable world.

The leadership potential of the Global South is not just determined by its economic power, but also by its distinct viewpoint on development, which is influenced by both resource constraints and the political and strategic use of resources, as well as environmental awareness. This perspective, coupled with a commitment to diversity and sustainability, offers a distinct path to a more just future. Countries like Brazil and India have made significant strides in renewable energy initiatives, demonstrating how sustainable development and economic prosperity can go hand in hand. These nations also demonstrate their leadership potential in addressing global issues through novel technological advancements that were misaligned in the past in agriculture and innovative healthcare solutions.

The Global South's leadership style might show a leaning toward an inspiring and unwavering commitment to sustainability, actively exploring and implementing alternative approaches to development, creating business ecosystems that foster entrepreneurship and attract foreign investment. They recognize the pivotal role of innovation and technological advancements in driving economic progress, which is evident in the proliferation of technology centers and the development of technology tailored to specific needs. By leveraging these advancements, the Global South has the potential to chart its course to success, bypassing traditional development trajectories. This Element intentionally omits certain leadership styles, such as democratic, authoritarian, or authoritative. Instead of thoroughly describing or analyzing their governance systems, the concept is left ambiguous. This approach allows readers the freedom to interpret and form their own opinions about the leaders' traits and the power dynamics within the narrative. By not providing explicit labels, a more nuanced and personalized understanding of the leadership and authority structures it presents is encouraged.

The Global South acknowledges the significance of having a cohesive voice and actively engaging in international forums that advocate for trade blocs. Global leadership relies on this aspect since it promotes a sense of solidarity and allows these countries to offer a more coherent position on matters that impact their progress. By collaborating, they magnify their collective effect, ensuring that their ideas are recognized and their problems are considered, understanding the power of working together to strengthen their influence and voice their concerns.

The ascent of the Global South to leadership heralds a promising shift toward a more just and equitable global order. It challenges the traditional Global

North-South divide by advocating for a future in which growth is a collaborative effort toward shared prosperity rather than a zero-sum competition. As said, this vision extends beyond economics to a future in which the Global South's ideas and experiences are valued and actively engaged in global discussions. In the end, the Global South is no longer a passive participant on the global stage. It actively pursues leadership positions to provide a new viewpoint to global challenges, expressing hope for a more egalitarian and environmentally conscientious society.

However, the road ahead, though challenging, is not insurmountable. With its internal heterogeneity and competing agendas, the Global South is an example of determination. Navigating the complex geopolitical terrain demands strategic collaboration and a willingness to compromise, qualities that the Global South is actively cultivating. Despite these constraints, the Global South's undeniable leadership potential shines through. Despite the absence of a singular leadership model, these nations possess the capability to redefine the global order, provided they wholeheartedly dedicate themselves to sustainable development, prioritize innovation, and effectively communicate with a united voice on an international level. While the Element shows a preference for a novel leadership style, it is worth noting that the emerging notion of leadership in the Global South may adopt a collective or shared leadership approach. These nations, while they do not have any one leadership style, possess the capacity to redefine the global power structure if they dedicate themselves to sustainable development, innovation, and an established cohesive global stance.

Appendices

Appendix 1. Description of Indices Used for GSL Index

Index	Description
Global Innovation Index (GII)	The GII reveals which countries are the most innovative in a given year of measurement and measures whether innovation drives productivity while also promoting economic growth. Higher scores indicate a larger productivity rate for a particular country. Switzerland had the highest rating while Guinea produced the lowest score of 11.6. The average index score resulted in a value of 32.09.
Global Sustainable Competitiveness Index	The Global Sustainable Competitiveness Index measures the competitiveness and sustainability of countries from 190 quantitative indicators. The 190 indicators are grouped into 6 sub-indices: Natural Capital, Resource Efficiency & Intensity, Social Cohesion, Intellectual Capital, Economic Sustainability, and Governance Efficiency. A higher score indicates that a country is performing better in terms of sustainable development, competitiveness, and overall well-being. The average sustainable competitiveness score in 2023 across all tested countries is 43.4 percent, and the highest score is 59.8, achieved by Sweden.
Global Economic Freedom Index	The Global Economic Freedom Index measures the impact of liberty and free markets regarding economic freedom within each country. The Index covers 12 freedoms including property rights and financial freedom for 184 countries. Higher scores are generally considered better. A higher score indicates greater economic freedom within a country, which typically correlates with factors such as lower government intervention, fewer restrictions on businesses, stronger property rights, and more open markets. Higher economic freedom scores are often associated with increased prosperity, higher standards of living, and greater opportunities for individuals and businesses to thrive.

(cont.)

Index	Description
Global Human Development Index (HDI)	The Global HDI is a composite index that measures the average achievement in three basic dimensions of human development: 1. Health (measured by life expectancy at birth) 2. Education (measured by mean years of schooling for adults aged twenty-five years and expected years of schooling for children entering school) 3. Standard of living (measured by Gross National Income per capita) The index calculates a geometric mean of standardized indices for each of the three dimensions. Higher scores indicate better development outcomes. Countries with higher HDI scores are considered to have higher levels of human development, including longer and healthier lives, better education, and higher standards of living. Conversely, lower HDI scores indicate lower levels of human development.
Global Marketing Potential Index (GMPI)	The GMPI is designed to assess the attractiveness of various countries as potential markets for international business expansion. The index ranks the market potential of the largest economies and provides guidance to the U.S. companies that plan to expand their markets internationally. Eight dimensions are selected to represent the market potential of a country and these factors include market size, economic growth prospects such as market intensity, market growth rate, market consumption capacity, infrastructure, regulatory environment, consumer behavior, and cultural factors. Higher scores indicate a greater potential for successful marketing opportunities and business growth within that particular country.
Global Happiness Index	The Global Happiness Index measures a nation's happiness and well-being levels among its citizens by implementing a statistical analysis of six categories. The six categories include GDP per capita, social support, healthy life expectancy, freedom to make your own life choices, generosity of the general population,

(cont.)

Index	Description
	and perceptions of internal and external corruption levels. Each happiness ranking represents a three-year average. A higher score indicates people in that country report higher levels of happiness and life satisfaction. Therefore, countries with higher scores on the Global Happiness Index are often viewed as having populations that are more content and fulfilled.
Global Peace Index (GPI)	The Global Peace Index measures the relative peacefulness of nations and regions around the world in about three domains. These three domains include the level of societal safety and security; the extent of ongoing domestic and international conflict; and the degree of militarization. In the GPI, low scores are better. The GPI measures the relative peacefulness of nations and regions around the world. A lower score indicates a higher level of peace, while a higher score indicates a lower level of peace or a higher degree of conflict and instability. Therefore, countries with lower scores in the GPI are considered more peaceful, while those with higher scores are considered less peaceful.
Global Education Index	The Global Education Index tracks and measures the average level of education in order to lend insight into the comparative educational development of countries around the world. In the Global Education Index, higher scores are typically better. Higher scores indicate better performance, quality, or access to education within a country or region while low scores generally indicate deficiencies or challenges in the education system, such as limited access to schooling, poor quality of education, or low levels of literacy and numeracy. Therefore, countries with higher scores are generally considered to have stronger and more effective education systems compared to those with lower scores.
Global Environmental Performance Index	The Global Environmental Performance Index ranks countries based on their environmental performance while considering various indicators such as air quality, water resources, and biodiversity among

(cont.)

Index	Description
	other factors. The index provides a quantitative basis for comparing, analyzing, and understanding environmental performance for 180 countries by using the most recent year of data and calculating how the updated scores changed over the previous decade. Higher scores indicate that a country is performing better in terms of environmental protection and sustainability, while a lower score suggests poorer performance. Therefore, countries with higher scores are typically considered to have better environmental performance compared to those with lower scores.
Global Health Security (GHS) Index	The GHS Index measures the capacities of 198 countries to prepare for epidemics and pandemics. The index notes that all countries remain dangerously unprepared for future epidemic and pandemic threats, including threats potentially more devastating than COVID-19. The average country score in the 2021 GHS Index was 38.9, a value consistently calculated for the years 2021 and 2019, and it shows continued weakness in global health security across all nations. Higher scores suggest that a country has better health outcomes, healthcare systems, infrastructure, and overall health-related indicators. Countries with higher scores are generally considered to be performing better in terms of public health, healthcare access, quality of care, disease prevention, and other relevant factors. Therefore, in most cases, a higher score on a global health index indicates a more favorable situation in terms of health and healthcare within a particular country.
Social Progress Index	The Social Progress Index measures various dimensions of social progress, including basic human needs, foundations of well-being, and opportunity. Involving 13 years of social progress data across 170 countries, the index concentrates on the non-economic aspects of global social performance in order to understand the true state of our society. Higher scores indicate better social progress. Therefore, a higher score indicates

(cont.)

Index	Description
	greater satisfaction with these needs, stronger foundations for well-being, and more opportunities available within a society. So, in the context of the SPI, higher scores are better.
Global Transparency Index	The Global Transparency Index measures a country's transparency accountability and integrity at all levels and across all sectors of society. The index provides information on identifying systems and networks that allow and permeate corruption throughout society. The average Global Transparency Index score remains at forty-three, indicating no real progress of persistent decline in corruption. Higher scores indicate greater transparency, accountability, and integrity in the practices of a country or organization. Conversely, lower scores suggest a lack of transparency and accountability, indicating areas where improvements are needed. Therefore, higher scores are generally preferred as they reflect stronger governance and better adherence to ethical standards.
Global Gender Gap Index	The Global Gender Gap Index measures the current state and evolution of gender parity across four key dimensions, which include economic participation and opportunity, educational attainment, health and survival, and political empowerment. The Global Gender Gap Index scores can be interpreted as the distance covered toward parity. The average global gender gap score in 2023 for 146 countries remains 68.4 percent. Higher scores indicate a smaller gender gap and are therefore better. The closer a country's score is to 100 percent, the smaller the gap between men and women in terms of economic participation and opportunity, educational attainment, health outcomes, and political empowerment.

Appendix 2. Subsection of Nine GSL Indices and GDP Per Capita

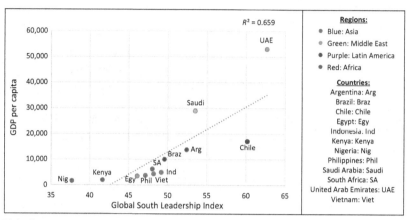

This figure was created by the authors based on information from Appendix 1 and World Bank DataBank.

Appendix 3. Subsection of Six Indices and GDP Per Capita

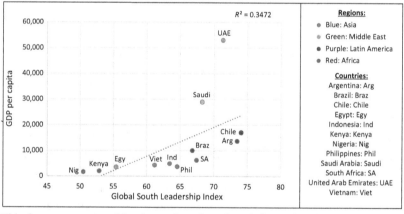

This figure was created by the authors based on information from Appendix 1 and World Bank DataBank.

Appendix 4. Subsection of Nine GSL Indices and PPP

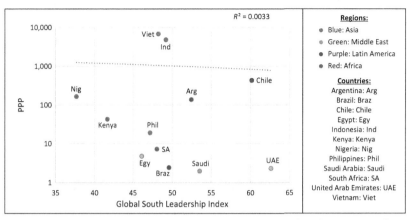

This figure was created by the authors based on information from Appendix 1 and World Bank DataBank.

Appendix 5. Subsection of Six GSL Indices and PPP

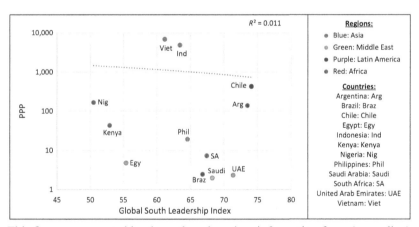

This figure was created by the authors based on information from Appendix 1 and World Bank DataBank.

Appendix 6. Subsection of Nine GSL Indices and Gini Coefficient

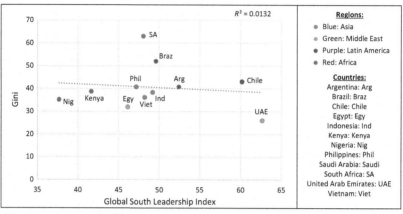

This figure was created by the authors based on information from Appendix 1 and World Bank DataBank.

Appendix 7. Subsection of Six GSL Indices and Gini Coefficient

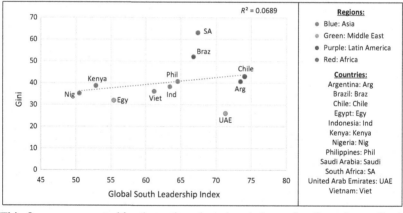

This figure was created by the authors based on information from Appendix 1 and World Bank DataBank.

Appendix 8. Subsection of Nine GSL Indices and GNI

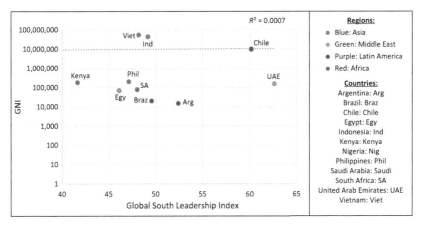

This figure was created by the authors based on information from Appendix 1 and World Bank DataBank.

Appendix 9. Subsection of Six GSL Indices and GNI

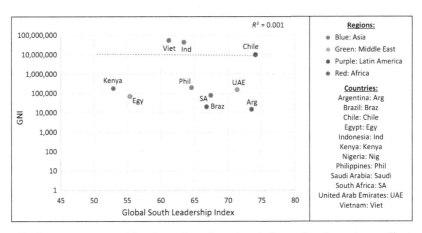

This figure was created by the authors based on information from Appendix 1 and World Bank DataBank.

Appendix 10. Breakdown of Leadership Styles and Perceptions in the Global South

Region	Possible GLOBE clusters	Dimensions	Leadership styles	Implicit and ideal leaders
Latin America	Hierarchal, egalitarian	Power distance (high/low), performance orientation (high/low)	Authoritarian, participative	Strong, decisive leaders with concern for employee well-being (varies by country)
Asia	In-group collectivism, Confucian dynamism	In-group collectivism (high), performance orientation (varies), future orientation (high/low)	Paternalistic, collectivistic	Benevolent leaders who prioritize group harmony and success (varies by country)
Africa	In-group collectivism, humane orientation	In-group collectivism (high), humane orientation (high), power distance (varies)	Communal, relationship-oriented leaders	Leaders who value social justice, fairness, and group welfare (varies by country)
Middle East	Future orientation, in-group collectivism	Future orientation (high/low), in-group collectivism (high), power distance (high)	Charismatic, assertive leaders	Visionary leaders who inspire and command respect (varies by country)

This table was created by the authors based on research information from House, R. J., Hanges, P. J., Javidan, M., Dorfman, P. W., & Gupta, V. (Eds.). (2004). *Culture, leadership, and organizations: The GLOBE study of 62 societies*. Sage publications.

Using the same list of countries that we have used throughout the Element analysis, the cultural leadership analysis for the Global South includes an examination of the 2004 GLOBE statistics with regard to the Global South countries in our analysis. This data comes from nearly 17,000 middle managers from 62 cultures who participated in the GLOBE project to better understand and assess cultural values and practices in their individual countries. The GLOBE study defines each country as having a distinct culture.

In the GLOBE study, researchers assessed and validated each country's score across nine cultural aspects. Country scores were determined for each country. Country scores were assigned to each culture dimension based on the values that it represents. The researchers were able to generate cluster ratings based on twenty-one major and six global leadership dimensions, which included cultural values, behaviors, and implicit leadership theory.

We ranked each of the twenty-seven aspects by the Global South country we utilized throughout our investigation to see if there are any commonalities in which dimension is more widespread and supported in the Global South countries. Then, we found the dimensions that produced the highest rankings for each country and compared the highest ranked dimensions from each country to one another.

The GLOBE study and our Element have nine Global South countries in common: Argentina, Egypt, Indonesia, Nigeria, the Philippines, South Africa (Black), South Africa (White), Taiwan, and Venezuela. As a result, we only considered these nations in our analysis of leadership trait dimensions. Integrity, Charismatic 2: Inspirational, and Performance-Oriented were identified as the leadership attributes with the greatest rankings across all of our Global South countries. Appendix 11 presents the rankings for each of these three aspects for all nine Global South countries, while Appendix 12 displays the average scores for each of these three dimensions for all nine Global South countries. Appendix 13 includes a scatter plot of average scores by country and dimension. The scatter plot shows how countries prioritize the top leadership attributes. Some cultures, such as South Africa (Black), undervalue these characteristics, while others, such as the Philippines, place a much higher value on all three dimensions: integrity, charismatic 2: inspiring, and performance-oriented.

Appendix 11. Leadership Traits for Chosen Countries

Rankings of countries by leadership characteristics	Integrity	Charismatic 2: Inspirational	Performance-oriented
Venezuela	3	4	1
Taiwan	2	4	6
Indonesia	2	3	1
Egypt	1	10	3
South Africa Black	5	2	3
South Africa White	1	2	6
Philippines	1	3	2
Argentina	4	1	2
Nigeria	1	4	3

Created based on GLOBE. (2004–2007). [GLOBE Phase 2 Aggregated Societal Level Data for Leadership Scales: May 17, 2004]. Retrieved from https://globeproject.com/study_2004_2007.html.

Appendix 12. Shared Traits That Underpin the Global South's Aspirations for Its Leaders by Ranking across the Chosen Countries

	Scores of countries by leadership characteristics	Integrity	Charismatic 2: Inspirational	Performance-oriented
1	Venezuela	5.89	5.81	6.05
2	Taiwan	5.89	5.74	5.67
3	Indonesia	6.34	6.29	6.36
4	Egypt	6.05	5.5	5.79
5	South Africa Black	5.36	5.56	5.47
6	South Africa White	6.35	6.33	6.01
7	Philippines	6.58	6.51	6.56
8	Argentina	6.15	6.32	6.2
9	Nigeria	6.07	5.98	6

Created based on GLOBE. (2004–2007). [GLOBE Phase 2 Aggregated Societal Level Data for Leadership Scales: May 17, 2004]. Retrieved from https://globeproject.com/study_2004_2007.html.

Appendix 13. Country Comparison of Leadership Traits

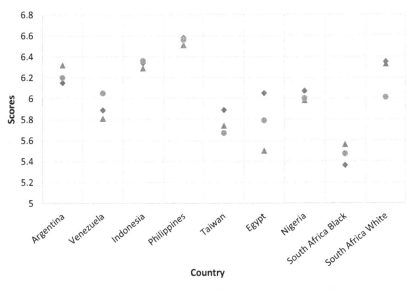

Created based on GLOBE. (2004–2007). [GLOBE Phase 2 Aggregated Societal Level Data for Leadership Scales: May 17, 2004]. Retrieved from https:// globeproject.com/study_2004_2007.html.

References

Adekola, A., & Sergi, B. S. (2016). Global business management: A cross-cultural perspective. Routledge.

Adrian, T., Gaspar, V., & Gourinchas, P.-O. (2024, Unknown Publish Date). The Fiscal and Financial Risks of a High-Debt, Slow-Growth World. IMF Blog. www.imf.org/en/Blogs.

African Business. (2023, June). The Future of the BRICS – in Conversation with Lord Jim O'Neill. https://african.business/2023/06/resources/the-future-of-the-brics-in-conversation-with-lord-jim-oneill .

Africanews. (2023, August 25). BRICS GDP to Grow by 36% Following Expansion. www.africanews.com/2023/08/25/brics-gdp-to-grow-by-36-following-expansion//.

AP News. (2024, June 14). UN: China Reaffirms Commitment to Global South at General Assembly. AP News. https://apnews.com/article/un-china-global-south-general-assembly-d8620e4502757c4de9ab41543f14eccb).

Arrighi, G., & Silver, B. J. (2005). Industrial Convergen Persistence of the N. Studies in Comparative International Development, 40(1), 83–88.

Avolio, B. J., & Yammarino, F. J. (2013). Transformational and Charismatic Leadership: The Road Ahead (Second edition, 10th anniversary edition., Vol. 5). Emerald Publishing Limited.

Bass, B. M., & Avolio, B. J. (1994). Improving organizational effectiveness through transformational leadership. SAGE.

Battle, S. (2024, January 12). This year's BRICS expansion points the way to the future for the world. Executive Intelligence Review, 51(2). https://larouchepub.com/other/2024/5102-brics_expansion_points_to_the.html

Bremmer, I. (2023, August 28). The New BRICS Expansion and the Global South Agenda. Blog post. www.gzeromedia.com/quick-take/the-new-brics-expansion-and-the-global-south-agenda.

Brummer, K. (2021). Advancing foreign policy analysis by studying leaders from the global South. International Affairs, 97(2), 405–421.

Caligiuri, P., & Tarique, I. (2012). Dynamic cross-cultural competencies and global leadership effectiveness. Journal of World Business, 47(4), 612–622.

Cele, S. (2024, January 31). BRICS gets a boost as Saudi Arabia joins a group of emerging nations. Bloomberg.

China US Focus. (2024, June 7). Can the Rising Global South Navigate the World of Great Power Rivalry? www.chinausfocus.com/foreign-policy/can-the-rising-global-south-navigate-the-world-of-great-power-rivalry.

Cobb, C., Halstead, T., & Rowe, J. (1995). The genuine progress indicator: Summary of data and methodology (Vol. 15). Redefining Progress.

Dabla-Norris, E., Gaspar, V., Poplawski-Ribeiro, M., & Yoo, J. (2024, May 10). Why Our World Needs Fiscal Restraint in Biggest-Ever Election Year. IMF Blog. www.imf.org/en/Blogs.

Dados, N., & Connell, R. (2012). The Global South. Contexts, 11(1), 12–13. https://doi.org/10.1177/1536504212436479.

Dai, M. (2024, April 2). Is BRICS offering an alternative model for global governance? East Asia Forum. https://eastasiaforum.org/2024/04/02/is-brics-offering-an-alternative-model-for-global-governance/.

Earley, P. C., & Mosakowski, E. (2004). Cultural intelligence. Harvard Business Review, 82(10), 139–146.

East Asia Forum. (2024, April 2). Is BRICS Offering an Alternative Model for Global Governance? https://eastasiaforum.org/2024/04/02/is-brics-offering-an-alternative-model-for-global-governance/.

Eden, D., & Leviathan, U. (1978). Implicit leadership theory: A conceptual framework for the study of leadership effectiveness. Journal of Management, 4(1), 7–17.

World Population Review. (2024). Education Index by Country 2024. https://worldpopulationreview.com/country-rankings/education-index-by-country.

EPI Results. (2022). EPI: Environmental Performance Index. Yale Center for Environmental Law & Policy. https://epi.yale.edu/epi-results/2022/component/epi.

Epitropaki, O., Sy, T., Martin, R., Tram-Quon, S., & Topakas, A. (2013). Implicit leadership and followership theories "in the wild": Taking stock of information-processing approaches to leadership and followership in organizational settings. The Leadership Quarterly, 24(6), 858–881.

Fellman, J., & Subramanian, A. (2024, April 8). Is India really the next China? Foreign Policy. https://foreignpolicy.com/2024/04/08/is-india-really-the-next-china/.

Foreign Policy. (2023, November 2). Israel-Palestine conflict: Hypocrisy and the Western response. Foreign Policy. https://foreignpolicy.com/2023/11/02/israel-palestine-hamas-gaza-war-russia-ukraine-occupation-west-hypocrisy/.

Foreign Policy. (2024). Can the Rising Global South Navigate the World of Great Power Rivalry? www.chinausfocus.com/foreign-policy/can-the-rising-global-south-navigate-the-world-of-great-power-rivalry.

Frayer, C. (2024, May 10). Why claims of deglobalisation are overblown [Blog post]. London School of Economics and Political Science Business Review. https://blogs.lse.ac.uk/usappblog/2024/05/11/why-claims-of-deglobalisation-are-overblown/.

Global Gender Gap Report 2023. (2023, June 20). World Economic Forum. www.weforum.org/publications/global-gender-gap-report-2023/.

World Intellectual Property Organization. (2022). Global Innovation Index 2022. www.wipo.int/global_innovation_index/en/

GLOBE. (2004–2007). GLOBE Phase 2 Aggregated Societal Level Data for Leadership Scales: May 17, 2004. https://globeproject.com/study_2004_2007 .html.

GNI per capita (constant LCU) by Country. Index Mundi (2019, December 28). www.indexmundi.com/facts/indicators/NY.GNP.PCAP.KN.

Gray, K., & Gills, B. K. (2016). South–South cooperation and the rise of the Global South. Third World Quarterly, 37(4), 557–574.

Group of 77 (G77). (2024). What Is the Group of 77? www.g77.org/.

Group of 77 (n.d.). About the Group of 77. www.g77.org/doc/.

Happiest Countries in the World 2024. World Population Review. https://world populationreview.com/.

Haug, S. (2021). A Thirdspace approach to the "Global South": insights from the margins of a popular category. Third World Quarterly, 42(9), 2018–2038. https://doi.org/10.1080/01436597.2020.1712999

Hofstede, G. (1980). Culture's consequences: International differences in work-related values. Sage.

Hofstede, G. (1991). Cultures and organizations: Software of the mind. McGraw-Hill.

House, R. J., Hanges, J. B., Javidan, M., Dorfman, P. W., & GLOBE Steering Committee. (2004). Culture, leadership, and organizations: The GLOBE study of 62 societies. SAGE.

House, R. J., Hanges, P. B., Javidan, M., Dorfman, P. W., & Gupta, V. (2004). Culture, Leadership, and Organizations:: The GLOBE Study of 62 Societies (1st ed.). SAGE.

Human Development Index. (2024, April 19). Human Development Reports. https://hdr.undp.org/data-center/human-development-index#/indicies/HDI.

The Heritage Foundation. (2023, October). Index of Economic Freedom: All Country Scores. www.heritage.org/index/ranking.

Institute for Economics & Peace. (2023, June). Global Peace Index 2023: Measuring Peace in a Complex World. http://visionofhumanity.org/resources.

International Food Policy Research Institute (IFPRI). (2022, March 2). War in Ukraine Blog Landing Page. www.ifpri.org/landing/war-ukraine-blog-landing-page.

International Monetary Fund (IMF). (2022, April 19). World Economic Outlook. www.imf.org/en/Publications/WEO/Issues/2022/04/19/world-economic-out

look-april-2022#:~:text=War%20slows%20recovery&text=Global% 20growth%20is%20projected%20to,percent%20over%the%medium%term.

International Monetary Fund (IMF). (2022, April 19). World Economic Outlook – April 2022: War Shadows the Global Recovery. www.imf.org/en/Publications/ WEO/weo-database/2022/April .

International Telecommunication Union. (2023). Measuring Digital Development: Facts and Figures 2023. www.itu.int/itu-d/reports/statistics/facts-figures-2023/.

James, N. (2024, February 12). Argentina's Populist Enigma: Javier Milei and the Rise of the Outsiders (2024, February 12). Council on Foreign Relations. www.cfr.org/americas/argentina.

Javidan, M., Dorfman, P. W., de Luque, M. S., & House, R. J. (2008). In-groups and out-groups in organizational studies. Academy of Management Review, 33(3), 598–614.

Javidan, M., Dorfman, P. W., De Luque, M. S., & House, R. J. (2017). In the eye of the beholder: Cross-cultural lessons in leadership from Project GLOBE. In Readings and cases in international human resource management (pp. 119–154). Routledge.

Jütten, M., & Falkenberg, D. (2024). Expansion of BRICS: A quest for greater global influence? (PE 760.368). European Parliamentary Research Service. Graphics by G. Macsai.

Kloß, S. T. (2017). The Global South as subversive practice: Challenges and potentials of a heuristic concept. Global South, 11(2), 1–17.

Kowalski, A.M. (2021). Global South-Global North Differences. In: W. Leal Filho, A. M. Azul, L. Brandli, A. Lange Salvia, P. G. Özuyar, T. Wall (Eds.), No Poverty. Encyclopedia of the UN Sustainable Development Goals. Springer. https://doi.org/10.1007/978-3-319-95714-2_68.

Laker, B. (2024, February 23). India to Become Third Largest Economy by 2027: Implications for Leaders. Forbes. www.forbes.com/sites/benjaminla ker/2024/02/23/india-to-become-third-largest-economy-by-2027-implica tions-for-leaders/.

López, A. J. (2007). Introduction: The (Post) Global South. The Global South, 1(1), 1–11. https://doi.org/10.2979/GSO.2007.1.1.1.

LSE Business Review. (2024, May 10). Why Claims of Deglobalisation Are Overblown. LSE Business Review. https://blogs.lse.ac.uk/businessreview/ 2024/05/10/why-claims-of-deglobalisation-are-overblown/.

Mahbubani, K., & Chatham House. (2024, February 2). Measuring the power of the Global South. Chatham House. www.chathamhouse.org/publications/ the-world-today/2024-02/measuring-power-global-south.

Mallick, M. G. P. K. (2024). Indian Strategic Studies. www.strategicstudyindia .com/2024/06/the-pivot-that-wasnt-did-america-wait.html.

Market Potential Index (MPI) – 2022. (2023, February 1). globalEDGE: Your Source for Global Business Knowledge. https://globaledge.msu.edu/mpi#changes2022.

McBain, W. (2023, May 26). Could a BRICS Currency Challenge the US Dollar? African Business. https://african.business/2023/05/trade-invest ment/can-brics-break-the-grip-of-the-greenback.

Mignolo, W. D. (2011). The Global South and world dis/order. Journal of Anthropological Research, 67(2), 165–188.

Miller, M. C. (2024, February 1). China and India Compete for Leadership of the Global South. Council on Foreign Relations. www.cfr.org/blog/china-and-india-compete-leadership-global-south.

Mitra, S. (2023, December 6). The False Promise of Import Substitution Industrialization in India. East Asia Forum. https://eastasiaforum.org/2023/12/06/the-false-promise-of-import-substitution-industrialisation-in-india-2/.

Nash, A. (2003). Third worldism. African Sociological Review/Revue Africaine de Sociologie, 7(1), 94–116. www.jstor.org/stable/24487379.

Papa, M., & Chaturvedi, R. (2024, April 2). Is BRICS Offering an Alternative Model for Global Governance? East Asia Forum. https://doi.org/10.59425/eabc.1712052000.

Papastergiadis, N. (2017). The end of the Global South and the cultures of the South. Thesis Eleven, 142(1), 69–90.

Patrick, S. (2023, August 15). The Term "Global South" Is Surging: It Should Be Retired. Carnegie Endowment for International Peace. https://carnegieen dowment.org/2023/08/15/term-global-south-is-surging.-it-should-be-retired-pub-90376.

Phiri, M. Z. (2017). Comparative perspectives on South Africa's and Brazil's institutional inequalities under progressive social policies. Journal of Southern African Studies, 43(5), 961–978.

Policy Center for the New South. (2023). The Rise of Global South: New Consensus Wanted. Annual Trends. www.policycenter.ma/publications/rise-glo bal-south-new-consensus-wanted.

Prahalad, C. K., & Hart, S. L. (1999). Strategies for the bottom of the pyramid: Creating sustainable development. Ann Arbor, 1001(1999), 48109.

Prashad, V. (2012). Dream history of the global South. Interface: A Journal for and about Social Movements, 4(1), 43–53

PricewaterhouseCoopers. (2017). The World in 2050: The Long View: How Will the Global Economic Order Change by 2050? www.pwc.com/gx/en/research-insights/economy/the-world-in-2050.html.

Qureshi, Z. (2023, May 16). Rising Inequality: A Major Issue of Our Time. Brookings Institution. www.brookings.edu/articles/rising-inequality-a-major-issue-of-our-time/.

Ta, R., Nguyen, T. L., Gupta, P., Chen, L., & Adeyemi, T. et al. (2023) Ai in the Global South: Opportunities and Challenges towards More Inclusive Governance, Brookings. www.brookings.edu/articles/ai-in-the-global-south-opportunities-and-challenges-towards-more-inclusive-governance/.

Rhodes, B. (2024). A Foreign Policy for the World as It Is. Foreign Affairs. www.foreignaffairs.com/united-states/biden-foreign-policy-world-rhodes.

Roland Berger. (2023). Global South: Beyond BRICS: Can the "Global South" Become the New Driver of Global Growth? www.rolandberger.com/en/.

Social Progress Imperative. (2024). Social Progress Index. www.socialprogress.org/2024-social-progress-index/.

The 2021 Global Health Security Index. (2023, December 5). GHS Index. https://ghsindex.org/.

The BRICS Post. (2024, March 10). BRICS Expansion: A New Dawn or a Dilution? https://thebraziliantimes.substack.com/p/the-new-dawn-of-brics-an-growing.1.

The Economist. (2024, April 12). Leaders | A realist's Guide: How to Locate the Global South. How a Fuzzy, Scorned Term Reflects Geopolitical Shifts. *The Economist*. www.economist.com/leaders/2024/08/12/how-to-locate-the-global-south.

The Economist. (2024, June 13). How Worrying Is the Rapid Rise of Chinese Science? The Economist. www.economist.com/leaders/2024/06/13/how-worrying-is-the-rapid-rise-of-chinese-science.

The Global Index. (2024, January 12). Global Sustainable Competitiveness Index. https://solability.com/the-global-sustainable-competitiveness-index/the-index.

The New York Times. (2023, February 27). Germany Announces Sharp Increase in Defense Spending after Ukraine Invasion [Correction: November 29, 2023]. The New York Times. www.nytimes.com/2023/11/29/world/europe/germany-military-strategic-pivot-stalls.html.

The South Centre. (2024). Board Members. www.southcentre.int/about-the-south-centre/.

Times Higher Education. (2024). Second-Chance Society: How Singapore Rethought Academic Success. www.timeshighereducation.com/.

Transparency International: The global Coalition against Corruption. (2024). Corruption Perceptions Index: Explore the Results. www.transparency.org/en/cpi/2023?gad_source=1&gclid=Cj0KCQjwzva1BhD3ARIsADQuPn

WXkYOynw1n0Viv3p0gpMcYP8erQdLqtkgzwxzuazp0zkt8rRAMYGkaAuo
vEALw_wcB.

United Nations Office for South-South Cooperation. (n.d.). UNOSSC. https://
unsouthsouth.org/.

United States – GINI Index. (World Bank estimate). (2019, December 28). Index
Mundi. www.indexmundi.com/facts/united-states/gini-index.

Vietnam – PPP conversion factor, GDP (LCU per international $). Index
Mundi (2019, December 28). www.indexmundi.com/facts/vietnam/ppp-con
version-factor.

Wagner, C. (2024, April 2). China's Universities Just Grabbed 6 of the Top 10
Spots in One Worldwide Science Ranking – without Changing a Thing. The
Conversation. https://theconversation.com/chinas-universities-just-grabbed-
6-of-the-top-10-spots-in-one-worldwide-science-ranking-without-changing-
a-thing-222956.

World Bank. (2023, January 10). Global Economic Prospects [Executive
Summary]. openknowledge.worldbank.org. https://openknowledge.world
bank.org/bitstream/handle/10986/38030/GEP-January-2023-Executive-
Summary.pdf.

World Bank. (2024, May 10). Nigeria Overview. www.worldbank.org/en/coun
try/nigeria.

Cambridge Elements ≡

Economics of Emerging Markets

Bruno S. Sergi

Harvard University

Editor Bruno S. Sergi is an Instructor at Harvard University, an Associate of the Harvard University Davis Center for Russian and Eurasian Studies and Harvard University Asia Center. He is the Academic Series Editor of the Cambridge *Elements in the Economics of Emerging Markets* (Cambridge University Press), a co-editor of the *Lab for Entrepreneurship and Development* book series, and associate editor of *The American Economist*. Concurrently, he teaches International Political Economics at the University of Messina, Scientific Director of the Lab for Entrepreneurship and Development (LEAD), and a co-founder and Scientific Director of the International Center for Emerging Markets Research at RUDN University in Moscow. He has published over 200 articles in professional journals and twenty-one books as author, co-author, editor, and co-editor.

About the Series

The aim of this Elements series is to deliver state-of-the-art, comprehensive coverage of the knowledge developed to date, including the dynamics and prospects of these economies, focusing on emerging markets' economics, finance, banking, technology advances, trade, demographic challenges, and their economic relations with the rest of the world, as well as the causal factors and limits of economic policy in these markets.

Cambridge Elements ⹀

Economics of Emerging Markets

Printed in the United States
by Baker & Taylor Publisher Services